KU-454-153

A BIRDWATCHING GUIDE TO
CYPRUS

ARTHUR STAGG
&
GRAHAM HEARL

ARLEQUIN

ISBN 1 900159 80 5

First published 1998

Arlequin Press, 26 Broomfield Road, Chelmsford, Essex CM1 1SW
Telephone: 01245 267771
© Arthur Stagg and Graham Hearl
© All illustrations James McCallum

All rights reserved. No part of this book may be reproduced, stored in a retrieval system or transmitted in any form or by any means, electronic, mechanical, photocopying or otherwise, without the permission of the publisher.

A catalogue record for this book is available.

C O N T E N T S

Central

Troodos Mountains area

Platres and Troodos paths and trails

Platres

Troodos

East

Larnaca area

Akhna and Cape Greco areas

Acknowledgements

The authors particularly wish to thank the Cyprus Ornithological Society (1957) for their comprehensive reports and newsletters which have enabled the systematic synopsis produced in this guide to reflect the status of species currently to November 1997. Finally very many thanks to Irene Hearl who produced the maps mainly from large scale maps of each area.

Introduction

Cyprus, or Aphrodite's Island as it is sometimes called, is approximately 225 km. long and 100 km. wide and is the third largest island in the Mediterranean after Sicily and Sardinia. It is tucked away at the extreme eastern end of the Mediterranean, some 75 km. south of Turkey and 115 km. west of Syria.

The island has suffered considerable strife in its long and chequered history and is currently in two enclaves following partition in 1974 after conflict between the Turkish Cypriot and Greek Cypriot elements of the population. The border separating The Turkish Republic of Northern Cyprus and The Greek Cypriot Republic of Cyprus is closed preventing visiting birdwatchers from moving freely between the two Republics.

Despite continuing simmering resentment between the two factions and occasional demonstrations a general calm prevails and this situation, which has existed since 1974, has not deterred millions of tourists from visiting the Greek Cypriot controlled area in complete safety in the intervening period. This guide has been written for those who wish to follow suit and enjoy the delights of this bird-rich island. It is a land which, following centuries of British influence, has English as a widely used second language, signs are in both Greek and English and vehicles drive on the left hand side of the road.

It is served by two international airports, Larnaca in the east and Paphos in the west, with numerous flights to and from Great Britain and Europe throughout the year.

A calendar of birds in Cyprus.

Cyprus with Turkey to the north, Syria to the east and Egypt to the south straddles one of the major migration flyways across the Mediterranean and is a staging post for many species which pass each year from Euro-Asia to Africa via the Nile delta. In consequence the Cyprus bird list is long; it currently stands at 363 species of which 48 are resident – including 14 endemics – and 40 or so migrant species which regularly or occasionally stay to breed.

Notable among the endemics and the resident species are Cyprus Warbler, Cyprus Pied Wheatear, Griffon Vulture and Black Francolin. Summer visitors include Eleonora's Falcon, Red-rumped Swallow, Black-headed Wagtail, Olivaceous Warbler, Masked Shrike, Cretzschmar's and Black-headed Buntings. In winter Flamingo and a wide variety of wildfowl are plentiful and Finsch's Wheatear is randomly seen.

Probably the best time to visit Cyprus is in spring when you may see not only resident and summer breeding visitors but also a selection of the island's many migrants in their more readily identifiable breeding plumages.

Spring migration starts in earnest in March when some winter visitors still linger. Thus as herons, hirundines, Great Spotted Cuckoo and some of the wheatears are arriving, a broad range of wildfowl, substantial numbers of Blackbird, thrushes and starling and perhaps a rare Pygmy Cormorant or an uncommon Armenian Gull may still be found. Later in March the first Roller, Red-rumped Swallow, Masked Shrike, Cretzschmar's Bunting and Black-headed Wagtail appear soon to be followed in early April by Olivaceous Warbler, Rüppell's Warbler and European Bee-eaters. It is also the time when the three species of black and white flycatchers arrive on the island and substantial flocks of Ortolan and Cretzschmar's Bunting abound. Later in April Black-headed Buntings arrive from Asia and quickly establish territories

Passerine migration, in the main, continues only until early May but a variety of waders may be found until the end of the month in locations where conditions are right and these could include Marsh Sandpiper, Collared and Black-winged Pratincole, Spur-winged Plover and Greater Sand Plover in addition to the more common Little Stint, Curlew Sandpiper and Ruff. April and May are good months for raptors such as Black Kite, harriers, Red-footed and Eleonora's Falcon and Hobby and perhaps, with luck, Osprey and Lesser Kestrel could come your way as well. Spring has other advantages: the island is usually verdant and flowers are in abundance. However the downside is that cool, overcast and wet weather is more likely.

Summer is mainly hot, dry and, in birding terms, quieter than the other seasons. Even so if you can stand the lowland heat the wetlands will still produce breeding/ over-summering herons and egrets and an assortment of waders, (including Spur-winged Plover), whilst in the cool of the mountains and foothills the endemic species plus others such as Alpine and Pallid Swift and the eye-catching Masked Shrike are readily to be found in surroundings of scenic beauty.

Autumn passage is less marked than that of spring and some species such as marsh terns, wagtails and wheatears can be difficult to separate in their juvenile or partially moulted adult plumages. However, there are alternative attractions such as the impressive movements of cranes and raptors which occur at this time of year. The Demoiselle Crane passes first in August and September and is followed by its congener the Common Crane during October and November. In some years thousands pass by day and night with many descending on to favoured locations such as the Akrotiri Salt Lake to feed and rest. Predominately during September there is also a considerable raptor passage with many of the buzzard and harrier species roosting overnight on the fringes of the Akrotiri Salt Lake providing superb close-up views in the early morning whilst they wait for thermalling conditions to develop or as they occasionally 'feel' the wind. At this time of year the Eleonora's Falcon have young in the nest and they are very active in the vicinity of their nesting cliffs and in their pursuit of travel-weary migrants; at this time too wader flocks are beginning to build. The autumn movement trickles on into November and almost imperceptibly merges with the arrival of winter visitors; indeed some of the autumn passage species winter as well which further blurs the transition.

Winter can be an excellent time for birdwatching in Cyprus, and with the tourist trade at its lowest ebb it is the time when accommodation and hire car bargains are to be found. Between November and March the Akrotiri and Larnaca Salt Lakes usually host thousands of Flamingo (with peak numbers in January) and a broad assortment of wildfowl, gulls and some waders too. It is the time of the year when many of the reservoirs are at their most productive, when you can look for Wallcreeper on coastal cliffs, Moustached Warbler and Bluethroat in the reedbeds, Finsch's Wheatear in general lowland locations and Little and Armenian Gull on coasts and wetlands. In winter there can be plenty of sunshine but equally it can be cold and wet. For sure though it will overall be warmer and drier than Europe and if it is exceptionally cold in the north you may find vagrant swans and geese joining you!

In all respects Cyprus is truly a year round birdwatching venue but for most visitors spring will have the edge.

Where to stay

Getting to Cyprus from the UK is relatively easy, there are international airports at both Larnaca in the south-east and Paphos on the west coast. Travel companies and agents in the UK all run typical package holidays to various resorts using both airports so the birder may take his pick.

The preferred accommodation of most visitors would seem to be an hotel on half-board basis, however, self-catering apartments are also readily available throughout the island and, for those on a limited budget or who prefer to roam at will, there are camping sites near to all the prime birdwatching locations; details of these are given under 'Camping Sites'.

There are three main birdwatching centres in Cyprus: Paphos on the west coast, Limassol in the centre of the south coast and Larnaca 75.0 km. further to the east.

The Paphos area has several good birding sites with the headland pre-eminent amongst these and highly recommended as an early morning and late afternoon venue. Apart from the local sites other good locations such as the Akamas Peninsula, Paphos Forest and the Troodos Mountains are within easy reach from the town, thus making Paphos an ideal birdwatching base.

Limassol likewise is a first class location from which to operate: it is close to the Akrotiri Peninsula which lies to the south-west of the town, it has fast connecting roads to Paphos, Troodos and Larnaca and even the Akamas Peninsula is within realistic reach, providing an early start is made.

The quality of birdwatching in the east of the island is variable and largely dependent on the level of water in Larnaca Salt Lake and its associated pools. In some years a 10 to 14 day holiday could productively be spent visiting and re-visiting the sites recommended in this guide, however in arid years as little as two to three days might well suffice. An ideal compromise would be to plan a two-centre holiday, staying a few days in the Larnaca or Ayia Napa areas but spending the preponderance of available birdwatching time in Limassol or Paphos. If a two-centre holiday is not an available option Limassol would be the best location from which to cover all the sites mentioned

For those who enjoy walking and who do not seek to maximise their Cyprus list the Akamas Peninsula is highly recommended. Development here has taken place to a degree sufficient to provide hotel and apartment accommodation, and even a camping site, whilst much of this rugged region remains unspoiled.

For those who prefer cool mountain air, beautiful views and walks through pine forest the tourist centres of Platres and Troodos are ideal although the bird species to be found are somewhat limited.

Camping Sites

All the sites listed provide parking, toilets, shower and washing facilities, piped drinking water, mini-market, cafe or restaurant. Two of the sites are open throughout the year these are No. 2. Governors Beach and No. 4. Feggari; the rest are open from spring until autumn. For details of charges and the exact opening and closing dates contact the sites direct.

Camping Site details	Capacity: caravans or tents
1. Ayia Napa Camping Tel. 03-721946 2.0 km. west of Ayia Napa	170
2. Governors Beach Camping Site P.O. Box 6152 Limassol Tel. 05-632300 20.0 km. east of Limassol	359
3. Geroskipou Zenon Gardens Geroskipou, Paphos P.O. Box 99 Tel. 06-242277 3.0 km. east of Paphos	95
4. Feggari Camping Pegeia-Paphos Tel. 06-621534 16.0 km. north of Paphos near Coral Bay	47
5. Polis Camping Polis Tel. 06-321526 1.0 km. north of Polis	200
6. Troodos Camping Facilities Tel. 05-421624 0.5 km. from Troodos to Pano Amiantos	170

Food and provisions

Most visiting birders tend to use hotel type accommodation with half-board but those staying in self-catering accommodation will find no shortage of supermarkets or shops in which to purchase provisions. Tavernas and restaurants are numerous and in the main provide good food at reasonable prices, though fish everywhere on the island is quite expensive. For those with healthy appetites a traditional kleftico- a succulent meat dish gently oven cooked for several hours – or a mezze – a variety of assorted dishes – are both highly recommended. Fish lovers will find swordfish steaks and red mullet good value. Cypriot food tends to be served with very few green vegetables but salads are a readily available alternative. A must for all is the toasted haloumi cheese, do try it.

Money and credit cards

The monetary unit is the Cyprus pound, Cy£, subdivided into 100 cents; the rate of exchange fluctuates but a reasonable guide for conversion is £10-00 = Cy£7-00. Most hotels and all banks and currency exchanges will change travellers cheques and bank notes but commission rates vary considerably making it worthwhile to shop around if time and opportunity permit; failing that a bank is the recommended option.

Most major credit cards are accepted in large stores and in many tavernas and restaurants; car hire can also be paid for by travellers cheque. Some cards are more popular than others but the Visa logo appears to feature more widely than any other.

Bank opening times vary from location to location depending on their volume of trade but all are open in the mornings from Monday to Friday, usually from 8.15 am to 12.30 pm. A growing number of banks also offer 24 hr. cashpoint services, accepting internationally recognised cards.

Getting around

Cyprus is a large island and the scattering of prime birdwatching sites makes it impractical for the visiting birder to get about other than by using a car or motorcycle. Much of the terrain to be covered is on unmade roads and tracks and four-wheel drive is best for several sites and imperative for others (as mentioned under birding sites) especially in the Akamas. However the use of a non four-wheel drive vehicle does not prevent access to any of the major sites but greater caution may be required and more footwork called for. Four-wheel drive vehicles generally cost 30% to 35% more to hire than conventional vehicles. Rates are keenly competitive and can often be negotiated lower especially if hiring for a week or longer. Beware of 'hidden' costs or extras such as collision damage waiver and make sure you see the full scale of charges especially if paying by credit card; remember reputable and reliable are the main criteria to follow when hiring vehicles abroad, especially when venturing into the 'backwoods'.

A current UK or other national licence is accepted by the Cyprus authorities.

Petrol and diesel are readily available but on Sundays many filling stations are not manned and fuel is obtained only via automatic dispensers which accept Cyprus currency notes of all denominations (they do not give change but do give tokens instead which can be used at same-brand filling stations). Note that there is no provision yet for the acceptance of credit cards at these automatic facilities but it is intended to incorporate this facility in due course.

For those that cannot or do not wish to drive there are buses which connect towns and villages and these can be used by those with more time to travel. Times of buses may be erratic, especially in villages, so it is best to enquire locally.

Service taxis run between major centres; this system, used in quite a few countries, is one of sharing a taxi with other people at a considerably lower tariff than is normally paid for private hire. If you want to use a service taxi enquire at your hotel or local bar for the location of the nearest collection point.

Bicycle hire is becoming increasingly available and is another means of covering many local sites.

Weather, clothing and skin protection

The climate of Cyprus is typically Mediterranean with long hot summers, cooler winters and changeable weather in spring and autumn. Consequently it is best to be prepared for all conditions taking shorts, tee-shirt and sun-tan lotion as well as wet-weather gear and something warm, especially for the mountains. Walking boots are recommended as the tracks can be very stony and rugged.

The mainly clear atmosphere of Cyprus results in the ultra-violet rays of the sun being largely unfiltered and skin burning can quite quickly occur, even on overcast days. Protection of the head from the sun and the use of barrier creams and lotions are common sense practices, also if you are not used to birdwatching in hot overseas locations beware of thin carrying straps on binoculars and cameras – they can bite into tender sunburnt skin and cause considerable discomfort. The use of broad straps on all optics suspended from the neck is recommended, placing the strap over clothing or a suitable pad.

You may also encounter insects as many of the prime birdwatching sites are rich in such pests, particularly mosquitoes in the wetter areas at certain times of the year and especially at dawn and dusk. Should you react to bites the use of a suitable insect repellent and an after-bite salve is recommended. Both are sold on the island should you forget to take them with you.

Use of optics in sensitive areas

In military zones and along the border between the Greek Cypriot and Turkish Cypriot enclaves there are notices and signs indicating photography is forbidden. Because of the difficulty at a distance in differentiating between a telescope and a long telephoto lens the use of all such equipment in sensitive areas is unwise. In proximity of military areas you may be stopped at any time and enquiries made about the purpose of your presence. Binoculars, telescopes and especially cameras will always attract attention so do not flaunt them.

Snakes in Cyprus

There are eight species of snake in Cyprus, three are venomous but only one is potentially dangerous to humans. This is the Blunt-nosed Viper *Vipera lebetina lebetina* which can be recognised by it's triangular-shaped head and a body of uniform thickness throughout it's length, terminating in a short, thin tail. This species is widespread and occurs in all types of terrain but is seen infrequently. The most commonly encountered snake is the Large Whip Snake *Coluber jugularis* (often called the Black Snake and known to locals as 'gardeners friend' because it eliminates rodents from orchards and deters other snakes) which is non-venomous and totally harmless, it is widespread and may sometimes be seen foraging around in holes in old olive and carob trees.

Snakes have poor sight, little hearing but a keen sense of smell – the tongue is the sensor. Human presence is likely to first be detected by vibrations caused by movement and if you are nervous of snakes it is not sensible to tip-toe through undergrowth in an attempt to avoid them. However when stalking birds in thick cover there is a need to move quietly so look before you tread and do not wear sandals or open-toed shoes. Likewise when scrambling over rocks and climbing over walls or logs look where you are placing your hands since snakes enjoy basking in early morning sunshine and may be sluggish if their body temperature is low. In the exceptionally unlikely event of being bitten by a snake try to note its colour and shape and seek medical attention immediately. Do not apply a tourniquet to the wound – it can do more harm than good – and do not consume alcohol which increases the blood circulation rate and the speed at which venom is spread

10

through the body.

Warning: A dead snake is not a safe snake. Even when dead or apparently dead snakes are capable of biting if touched, possibly due to some reflex action, so do not handle out of interest or curiosity!

Other general points

The native language is Greek but due to the long English presence on the island English is spoken by many Greek Cypriots especially in the main towns and tourist resorts.

The Cyprus Ornithological Societies – means of contact

Confusingly there are two ornithological societies on the island and both are named 'Cyprus Ornithological Society'. One was formed in 1957 by British military personnel serving in Cyprus and throughout its life has enjoyed the support of Cypriots and other nationals. This society has a large membership, a dedicated and active committee, has regular field meetings and produces both a monthly newsletter, which gives details of species seen during the period, and a comprehensive annual report. The society maintains a Bird Information Centre, which is currently located in the Apollo Hotel at Kato Paphos, and this is manned daily by COS members from 10-30 am to 12-30 pm during migration periods. The Cyprus birdline, operated by the society, is active throughout the year and it is currently contactable by telephone on 06 -233707.

COS (57) welcomes news of rare or interesting sightings either via the 'hotline' or in person at the Bird Information Centre; likewise the society is keen to receive records of visitors sightings supported by field notes for rare and vagrant species and these should be sent to Cyprus Ornithological Society (1957), Yiangou Souroulla 6, CY-6037, Larnaca, Cyprus, Tel/Fax No. 04 651002.

The second Cyprus Ornithological Society -(COS 70)- was formed in 1970 and controls all bird ringing activities on the island. This society may currently be contacted by telephone on 02 42073, by Fax No 02 493689 or by writing to Cyprus Ornithological Society, ICBP Cyprus, 4 Kanaris Street, Strovolos 2059, Cyprus.

Using this guide

This guide is designed for the visiting birdwatcher with limited time who wishes to cover the best of the accessible sites. Despite the fact that there are known 'hotspots' it is worth remembering that the whole island straddles a major migration flyway and in adverse weather conditions falls of migrants may occur almost anywhere. In such circumstances any habitat near the coast, whether mentioned in this guide or not, may be brimming with migrants and should not quickly be forsaken in favour of heading for one of the named locations.

A good map such as the 'Road & Tourist Map of Cyprus' published by SELAS Ltd. P.O.Box 8619, Nicosia, Cyprus (available in many shops and supermarkets in Cyprus) used in conjunction with this book should get you to the best sites.

The scientific names of bird species mentioned in the text are given in the checklist at the back of this guide.

The system of numbers given in the black circles on several of the maps cross-refer directly to the numbers in the text for the relevant site.

For reference purposes Map 1 gives a general picture of Cyprus showing the two main airports, the location of the major towns, and the best birding areas as detailed in this guide.

N.B. The double dotted lines on the maps indicate tracks which are sometimes passable by vehicle and sometimes not, dependent on the effects of weather.

Finally please bear in mind that details of sites and, more particularly, access to sites is subject to change as island-wide development continues.

11

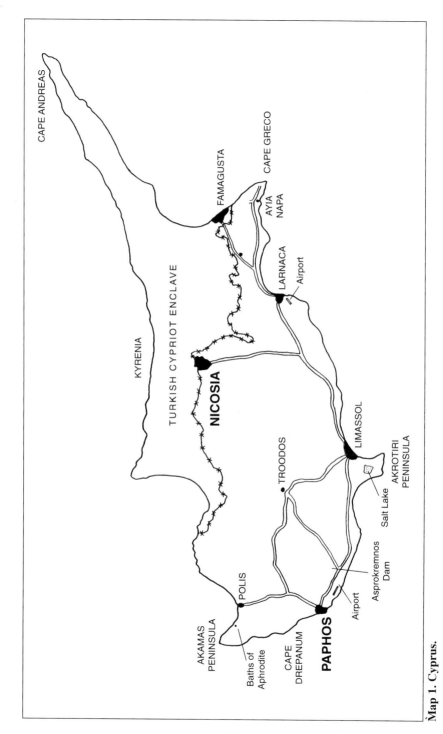

CAPE ANDREAS

FAMAGUSTA

CAPE GRECO

AYIA NAPA

KYRENIA

TURKISH CYPRIOT ENCLAVE

LARNACA

Airport

NICOSIA

•TROODOS

LIMASSOL

AKROTIRI PENINSULA

Salt Lake

Asprokremnos Dam

Airport

POLIS

AKAMAS PENINSULA

Baths of Aphrodite

CAPE DREPANUM

PAPHOS

Map 1. Cyprus.

12

Birding Sites in Cyprus (Map 1)
Central South
The Akrotiri Peninsula (Map 2)

The Akrotiri Peninsula is the southernmost promontory of the island and is situated south-west of the town of Limassol. The habitats on this peninsula are extremely varied and include tall craggy cliffs, sand and pebble beaches, a salt lake, marshland, reedbeds, stands of eucalyptus, citrus groves, arable land, scrub and sundry pools which hold water throughout year. With this wide variety of habitats it is not surprising that the area is a magnet for birds migrating northwards in spring and southwards in autumn, as well as harbouring a wide range of wintering species.

The Akrotiri Peninsula is also the long term home of a large British Military Base. For security reasons certain areas are off-limits to non-service personnel but, other than the Akrotiri cliffs which host a large breeding colony of Eleonora's Falcon, fortunately all the prime sites are freely accessible.

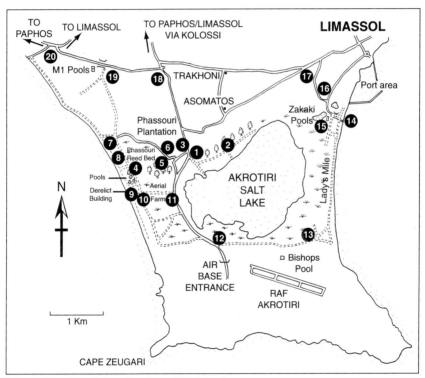

Map 2. The Akrotiri peninsula and Episkopi area.

1. The Akrotiri reedbeds

Travelling from Limassol the Akrotiri Peninsula can be reached via a variety of major and minor roads. If travelling from the direction of Paphos on the B6/A6 road it is recommended you leave the motorway at the second signpost to Erimi and then follow the clearly marked route to Akrotiri via Kolossi. Thereafter, irrespective of the direction of approach to Akrotiri, all ways converge on the road which runs south through the Phassouri Plantation towards the Air Base.

To reach the reedbeds, which fringe the north-western shore of the Akrotiri Salt Lake,

13

follow the road through the plantation until you come to a sharp right-hand bend, slow down and once through the bend turn immediately left down a track signposted 'Forest Nursery Fasouri' ❶. There are turns off this track both left and right but best results in all seasons are likely to be achieved by following the main track for approximately 1.0 km. until it intersects with a cut-through to the edge of the salt lake ❷. On the left of the track are eucalyptus trees backed by citrus groves; Serin are present in abundance the year round and in spring and autumn the eucalyptus trees harbour Golden Oriole and roosting raptors. The reedbeds to the right of the track can be dense and up to 5 m. high, (although in 1997 they had been burned to the ground) and ring to the staccato chatter of Cetti's Warbler; in winter Moustached Warbler and Bluethroat are plentiful and Penduline Tit may occasionally be found.

The cut-through on the right to the Salt Lake can be treacherously soft and impassable even to four-wheel drive vehicles but it is well worth walking if conditions allow.

Between here and westwards to the military aerial farm bordering the Akrotiri road, Dead Sea Sparrow were, in 1980, found breeding in the area where the reeds thin and intermingle with tamarisk. Thereafter they were seen regularly for several years between March and November but their status today is uncertain; even so this site with its ideal habitat provides the best chance of connecting with this elusive Cyprus rarity. Spectacled Warbler also breed here and, depending on water levels, the area can be very good for Spotted and Little Crake and occasionally Baillon's Crake, mainly in spring but sometimes in autumn as well.

2. Phassouri reedbeds

To get to the Phassouri reedbeds return to the plantation road, turn right and take the next road left ❸, turn right at the subsequent tee junction then follow the road round to the left. Resist the temptation to birdwatch as you drive on this stretch since it is narrow and twisting and much used by briskly moving farm vehicles. Once through the last bend the reedbeds ❹ can be seen ahead to the left of the road beyond grassland which becomes a water meadow in winter and remains so into spring. To the east of the reedbed, extending to the road, an extensive stand of eucalyptus ❺ marks the eastern boundary of the Phassouri reedbeds. The best way to cover this area, and especially when the grassland is waterlogged, is to pull off the road onto dry ground and birdwatch from your vehicle ❻.

In spring an abundance of Squacco Heron, Little and Cattle Egret, Glossy Ibis, Ruff and Wood Sandpiper will often feed unconcernedly within feet of birdwatchers, with multi-race groups of Yellow Wagtail and Red-throated Pipit interspersed among them. For those wishing to explore on foot the eucalyptus grove provides ample parking space, and a clockwise walk to the rear of the reedbed (underfoot conditions permitting) may well reveal crakes in some of the runnels and give views of Little Bittern and Night Heron in the reeds.

3. Akrotiri gravel pits

To cover the Akrotiri gravel pits area return to the road from the Phassouri reedbeds and proceed northwest in the general direction of Kensington Cliffs which are visible in the distance. Turn left at the first tee junction ❼, on to a rather rough all-weather road which turns to run south parallel with the south west aspect of the Phassouri reedbeds through low scrub and stunted bushes. 1.0 km. after the left turn there is a subsidiary track ❽ to the right which leads to a stony shore; the condition of the track varies from season to season and is usually best suited to four-wheel drive vehicles. At the shore the track converges with another which is considerably rougher and runs south-east towards Cape Zeugari and north-west to Curium beach. The barren shoreline attracts few birds but offshore rafts of duck gather in this area in winter and in early spring; the point where the tracks converge can be extremely good for Spectacled Warbler.

Just after the shoreline turn there is a series of pools close by the side of the road; these continue for about 700 m. in a south-east direction before terminating at another right-hand turn which leads past derelict buildings **9** to the sea. This is an excellent place at which to stop and check the pools, the scrub and the bushes as many inbound and outbound migrants are frequently to be found here. In the past it has proved to be especially good for Sparrowhawk, Red-footed Falcon. Hobby, pipits, wagtails, wheatears, warblers and shrikes.

To the south-east of the derelict buildings are several mud tracks which can, as the many wheel ruts show, be soft and treacherous after rain. It is best therefore when leaving the area to return to the all-weather road, turn right and 300 m. ahead turn left **10** and continue for 1.8 km. through the aerial farm to join the Akrotiri road at **11** a point 1.0 km. north of the start of Akrotiri village.

NB. Do NOT attempt to photograph birds when passing through the aerial farm which falls within a military zone

Collared Flycatcher

4. Akrotiri Salt Lake
The lake when full covers an area of approximately 9.0 sq. km. and in winter, usually commencing in November, hosts several thousand Greater Flamingo and various species of wildfowl and gull.

The ideal conditions for birding occur when the lake is less than full leaving damp margins attractive to waders. Particularly good under these conditions are the southern sector and the eastern track known as Lady's Mile incorporating Zakaki marsh. In autumn the Salt Lake is a regular stop-over and roosting area for Demoiselle Crane, which occurs from late August to early September sometimes in hundreds, and its congener the Common Crane which follows in thousands during October and November. Their return during March and April is less noticeable with most overflying the island. Raptors, predominately buzzard species, are also a notable autumn feature of the Salt Lake, passing through mainly in September and early October when many roost overnight on the fringes of the Salt Lake as well as in the eucalyptus trees which border the Akrotiri reedbeds on the northern edge of the lake. They depart early to mid morning as thermalling conditions develop.

5. Lady's Mile
The approach track to Lady's Mile is situated on a rising curve in the road, just short of the Air Base entrance, immediately after and partially obscured by the Sylvana Restaurant **⑫**. This elevated turning point affords one of the best, albeit distant, views of the salt lake and the thousands of Greater Flamingo which gather there in winter. Early morning is the best time of the day to visit the lake before the heat haze develops and distorts vision.

The track skirts the southern edge of the lake and, after 200 m., passes a cat sanctuary housing 60+ felines so please drive carefully. The track then continues with uninterrupted views across the lake and its surrounds for a further 1.6 km. before entering an avenue of wattle and eucalyptus trees; during spring migration the wattles in particular attract Pied, Semi-collared and Collared Flycatchers. At 2.6 km. the track passes the entrance to Bishop's Pool (once a notable birding spot but now closed to the general public) and continues through the avenue of trees for a further 800 m. before passing an observation tower on the left and breaking out on to the south-east edge of the salt lake **⑬** . It is here that excellent early morning views of ground-roosting raptors can be obtained during their September/October passage.

At this point three main tracks cross the lake, Lady's Mile can be reached by taking the right hand or centre track; drivers should note that, although this portion of the track is usually firm enough for vehicles, caution is merited in wet conditions.

At Lady's Mile turn north towards the cranes of Limassol Port visible in the distance. The sea is on the east of the track largely screened from view, but to the west of the track there are pools and stretches of moist sand which are much favoured by waders, notably Marsh Sandpiper, Greater Sandplover, Sanderling and Broad-billed Sandpiper. On the seaward side there are five beach bar/restaurants which serve sea-food and provide excellent watchpoints from which to observe migrant traffic.

6. Zakaki marsh and pools
Zakaki marsh is reached by continuing north along Lady's Mile and bearing left at the Oasis Bar **⑭** , across a mini-causeway and past a somewhat ramshackle football stadium **⑮** , Zakaki pools are 300 m. beyond the stadium. Here the track converts to a tarmac road to the south-west of which is the main expanse of marsh with its associated pools. The development of Limassol Port has in recent years encroached on and reduced the area covered by Zakaki marsh. Despite this reduction in area it remains a prime birding site, especially in winter and spring, but it is often underrated by visiting birders. The large pool on the west side of the road is excellent in spring for Garganey, Whiskered and White-winged Black Terns, Collared and Black-winged Pratincole, whilst the ooze generated around the edges as the marsh dries attracts waders of many species in substantial numbers especially Little Stint, Curlew Sandpiper, Ruff, Marsh and Wood Sandpiper and sometimes Broad-billed Sandpiper. The marsh also attracts Glossy Ibis, Squacco Heron and Black-winged Stilt in good numbers. There is a smaller pool to the east of the road but this is less attractive to migrants.

Plate 1. Akrotiri Salt Lake taken from the south side illustrating the vast nature of this area and the extent of the salt margins which vary from season to season.   *Graham Hearl*

Plate 2. Phassouri reedbeds with the fields in the foreground which, when flooded create a superb habitat for a variety of wetland species but especially Squacco Heron, Glossy Ibis and waders.
Graham Hearl

Plate 3. *Zakaki pools. This area of pools and marsh at the north-east corner of Akrotiri Salt Lake is a favourite haunt of herons, egrets, waders and marsh terns.* Arthur Stagg

Plate 4. *M1 pools. Well worth checking for Little Bittern, Night Heron and waders.*
Arthur Stagg

Plate 5. Quarry beach and Kensington Cliffs. Kensington Cliffs are the breeding site of Griffon Vultures which may often be seen from this point above Quarry beach. The scrub in the foreground is also very good for Cyprus Warbler.   Arthur Stagg

Plate 6. Asprokremnos Dam and pools. The area with pools in the foreground under the dam wall is one of the prime birding sites in Cyprus.   Graham Hearl

Plate 7. *The Dhiarizos Valley, just north-east of Asprokremnos Reservoir, which leads up into the Troodos Mountains.*
Graham Hearl

Plate 8. *The foothills of the Troodos Mountains: ideal habitat for Long-legged Buzzard.*
Arthur Stagg

Note

Zakaki marsh is an excellent site at which to photograph birds from the roadside whilst using the car as a mobile hide.

To return to the starting point of the circuit of prime Akrotiri Peninsula bird sites continue north for approximately 1.0 km. and turn left at the traffic lights **⑯** . A further 1.0 km. along this road turn left at a Petrolina filling station **⑰** and head west through Asomatos to the Phassouri Plantation. 300 m. from the filling station is Vavatsiniotas Super Store – a very competitively priced outlet for a wide range of foodstuffs, beverages and the like.

For those heading towards Limassol from Zakaki or travelling further eastwards turn right at the Petrolina filling station and follow the clearly marked road signs.

Depending on holiday venue and sun position relative to time of day it may be preferred to commence the circuit in reverse, from Zakaki, in which case follow the Zakaki road and turn south on the road signposted 'Lady's Mile' **⑰** at the Petrolina station.

Other sites

1. Limassol Dams

To the north of the town of Limassol there are three dams which vary in their attractiveness to birds depending on water level and season. Generally they are most productive from late autumn through winter and into spring when passage migrants pause to rest and recoup, and other species take up winter residence.

The dams are all adjacent to the town's new bypass road. The main route to the Kouris Dam – the largest dam on the island – is from the western boundary of the town near Ypsonas; the road is well signposted. The Polemedhia Dam however is not signposted but may be found by connecting with the B8 Limassol to Troodos road approximately midway along the bypass and following that road north for 3.5 km. before turning off the road on the brow of a hill just beyond a small red-roofed church. The Yermasoyia Dam (sometimes spelt Germasoyia) is reached by leaving the bypass, Limassol to Nicosia road, at junction 24 on the east side of the town and following the signs.

The Kouris Dam has a well established reedbed on the south side of the wall of the dam. In spring this area attracts Night Heron, Purple Heron, Little Bittern and Great Reed Warbler; in late autumn and winter look for Bluethroat and Moustached Warbler. Throughout the year the Rock Dove colony located in the surrounding cliffs draws Peregrine Falcon.

The Polemedhia Dam is well stocked with fish and is worth checking from autumn to spring for both Great Crested Grebe and Pygmy Cormorant.

The Yermasoyia Dam is the best of the Limassol dams. It is easily accessible, has a range of good viewpoints and has a record for producing the irregular and unusual. White Stork, Black Stork and White Pelican have occurred here, Great Crested and Black-necked Grebe are regular in winter along with sundry wildfowl. Nearby is the village of Akrounda and here there is a stream bed which is worth checking for Water Rail and crake species.

Episkopi area (Map 2)

For the purpose of this guide the Episkopi area extends from midway along the M1 road - a fast section of highway which starts just north of the Phassouri plantation and connects with the Limassol to Paphos road west of Episkopi village – and continues westward as far as Avdimou Melanda beach. The area incorporates a variety of habitats ranging from fertile coastal plain, largely made over to viniculture, pebble and sand beaches, scrubland, eucalyptus stands and steep limestone cliffs covered with dense growths of cistus. The avifauna it hosts is as varied as the habitats and includes herons, egrets, duck, a variety of raptors, waders and various passerines. The whole area is located within what is termed the Western Sovereign Base Area, a sector within which there is a range of British Military facilities. Because of the military presence some parts are out of bounds to the general

21

public but even so there is much to see in the sites covered.

When leaving the Akrotiri peninsula via the Phassouri plantation to travel westward take the first road to the left ⓲ towards Curium, this is known as the M1 and it intersects with the Limassol/Paphos road ⓴ adjacent to the Curium Beach turn. The overhead wires bordering the road attract migrant Roller, and falls of Red-footed Falcon sometimes gather here in autumn.

The sites worth covering in this area are:-

1. M1 pools
At approximately the midway point towards Curium (Kourion) the M1 crosses a road bridge, turn off the road just before the bridge and park ⓳ . Diagonally west there is a man-made pool backed by fir trees. On its southern aspect and adjoining it is an overflow area surrounded by an earth bund, this spot is much favoured by waders. It is also a favourite haunt of the hunting fraternity during the shooting season as evidenced by the large number of spent shotgun cartridges littering the ground. The trees behind the pool attract Night Heron, the reeds are good for Little Bittern and the occasional crake, and the shallow pools support a wide variety of waders and many other species which use the pool to drink and bathe.

2.Curium beach and cliffs
Continue along the M1 and turn left where the road meets with the Limassol-Paphos intersection ⓴ and almost immediately turn left again onto a road which passes St. Ermogenis restaurant on the right; this road leads to the beach.

To the south of Curium beach a rough track follows the shoreline and eventually connects with the Akrotiri gravel pits. This area attracts Stone Curlew, wheatears and pipits. The track to the west leads past three beach bar/restaurants to terminate in the lea of a cliff just past the Sunshine Restaurant. Here there is a seasonal damp area with reeds, trees, bushes and scrub which are well worth checking for migrants, but the prime attraction of this area is the good view often obtained of Griffon Vulture, Peregrine and Eleonora's Falcon as they move to and from their nearby breeding sites.

3. Kensington Cliff viewpoint
To reach the viewpoint return to the Limassol-Paphos road, turn left and continue up a steep winding hill and on towards the Sanctuary of Apollo. From pull-offs to the left of the road there are fine views of the southward sweep of Akrotiri Peninsula and the cistus and lentisc here harbour a large concentration of Cyprus Warbler. Just beyond the entrance to the Sanctuary of Apollo, which is on the right, there is a turning left which leads downhill on a rough unmade road to Quarry beach and from here Kensington Cliff - the breeding ground of the local populations of Griffon Vulture and Eleonora's Falcon- can be scanned.

4. Avdimou – Melanda beach
Melanda beach in the Avdimou valley can be reached from the Kensington Cliff viewpoint either by remaining on the old Limassol to Paphos road passing through Paramali or by rejoining the B6/A6 motorway and heading towards Paphos at Paramali, just beyond the Episkopi garrison boundary. The Melanda beach turn is 13.5 km. from the Kensington Cliff viewpoint when using the latter route. The turning, on the left hand side of the road, is 1.4 km. from the Avdimou exit on the motorway and is marked by a red and white board advertising the Melanda Beach Restaurant. The track to the beach passes through unspoiled countryside largely given over to cereal crops and viniculture and dotted here and there with olive and carob trees. The valley can be a veritable haven for downed migrants in bad weather and the terrace of the beach restaurant is an excellent spot from which to observe over-the-sea movements.

Irrespective of the birding attractions this unspoilt valley is worth a visit to be reminded of the beauty of this coast in pre-development days. The restaurant serves excellent fish meals at reasonable prices.

Note.

There are three camp sites at Melanda beach but they are exclusively for use by military personnel.

South west

Paphos area

For the purpose of this guide the Paphos area is regarded as extending for an approximate 25.0 km. radius of the town of Paphos and comprises a many and varied range of habitats. On the south-eastern boundary tall limestone cliffs abut the sea, providing breeding sites for a number of species; further westward the cliffs give way to a coastal plain which comprises an admix of scrub and farmland, of stony beaches, rocky foreshores and occasional sandy bays, before rising again to form a cliff-fringed littoral, again backed by scrubland and cultivated fields amongst which, especially beyond Paphos, are many banana plantations.

Paphos itself is a town which has grown rapidly and extensively in recent years (and indeed is still growing) and here Greco-Roman ruins mix and mingle with modern-day dwellings, shops and the like. However the headland between the port and the lighthouse is, as yet, undeveloped and its grassland, fringed by bushes and trees and by many ancient ruins, which lie to the rear of the rocky coast, are a veritable haven for a wide variety of migrants and provide an ideal observation point for coasting flocks of herons, egrets etc. This general area has produced many rare and unusual sightings over the years.

Instructions for reaching the various sites commence from the previously described Episkopi area. Accordingly continue to move west along the Limassol-Paphos road from Avdimou to reach the next site of interest which is Cape Aspro.

Eleonora's Falcon

23

1. Cape Aspro

Cape Aspro is so called because of its sheer white cliffs which face onto the sea. The cape is beyond Pissouri approaching Petra tou Romiou (often called 'Aphrodites Rock') and the cliffs here hold one of the largest colonies of Eleonora's Falcon on the island as well as Alpine Swift, Shag, Cormorant and Rock Dove.

The access to the beach and cliffs is via an underpass situated close to a layby on the northern side of the road. The road here is on a steep incline and is often busy with fast moving traffic. Consequently it is not recommended that those travelling in a westerly direction pull across the oncoming traffic to park in the layby, it is better by far to carry on to the Petra tou Romiou Tourist Centre (perhaps taking advantage of the facilities there) and back-track the 2.5 km. to the layby.

The underpass access is found by descending a track at the side of the road 15 m. west of the layby. During migration periods, especially in spring, the bushes on the seaward side of the underpass can be good for passerines, warblers and shrikes in particular.

2. Kouklia

10.0 km. from Cape Aspro, heading towards Paphos, there is a signboard indicating Kouklia, Archimandreta and Dora (F612) to the right of the road with Timi and Paphos straight ahead (B6). 800 m. further on, just after an 80.0 km. sign and before a line of fir trees, is a track to the left which passes close by an old stone bridge and meanders through farmland for about 2.0 km. towards the sea. The area is particularly good for Stone Curlew and at the seaward end of the track there are reedbeds, bushes and seasonal pools which attract a broad range of migrants, particularly pipits, wagtails and warblers.

3. Asprokremnos Dam and pools (Map 3)

Returning to the road along the Kouklia track turn left, 1.0 km. further on is a sign pointing right to Ayios Nikalaos and Platres (F616), the turning is 300 m. ahead just before a bridge; across the bridge is a further turning right ❶ which leads to the Asprokremnos Dam. (This turning is also alerted 1.2 km. before the turn in both directions). Take this turn and, after 600 m., turn right ❷ at an unmade road passing contractors buildings on the left hand side. Follow the track in the direction of the wall of the dam to reach reed-fringed pools on the left ❸; these pools are filled by rainfall and by water periodically released from the reservoir; their productivity in birding terms varies depending on the level of water they contain. They occasionally host Baillon's Crake but more frequently Little Crake and Water Rail as well as Little Bittern, various egrets and herons, and a variety of waders. The bushes and scrub near the pools hold a variety of warblers on migration and on the cliffs above the pools Little Owl, Kestrel and Rock Dove breed.

Return to the road and turn right up a steep incline to cross over the dam ❹; from here the reservoir may be scanned for wildfowl and marsh terns, and in winter months for grebes and cormorants, including Pygmy Cormorant.

For those with time to spare a visit to the northern end of the reservoir could prove worthwhile since Pied Kingfisher has in the past been seen in this less accessible area. To reach it cross the dam and turn left at the tee junction; 700 m. further on is a sign indicating a left turn ❺ to Kholetria/Choletria (F617) which is a village some 6.0 km. ahead. Take this road, continue on beyond Kholetria for a further 1.7 km. and turn left ❻ onto a part graded, part stone block road which leads west to Nata. Much of the land here is made over to cereals and grass and holds resident populations of Fan-tailed Warbler and Corn Bunting whilst Black-headed Bunting are numerous from late April till late May; Bonelli's Eagle has also been recorded on occasions between here and Nata.

2.7 km. along this road is a shallow water splash crossing the Xero Potomas river which feeds the Asprokremnos Dam; 1.0 km. further the road divides right to Nata and left to Anarita, Timi and Paphos; take the left fork and 100 m. ahead to the left, opposite a concrete water tank perched on a mound, is a narrow unmarked dirt track ❼ which ultimately leads to the abandoned village of Phinikas(Finikas) ❽ on the western side of

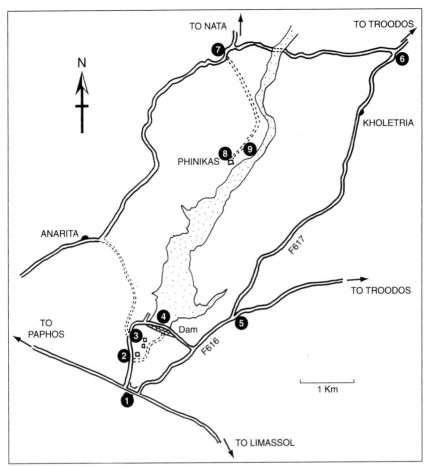

Map 3. Asprokremnos Dam and pools.

the reservoir. The reservoir shallows ❾ attract herons, egrets, waders and the occasional Pied Kingfisher but unless a four-wheel drive vehicle is used this diversion could prove to be a time-consuming footslog for little reward, so perhaps it would be best to check with the C.O.S. birdline for recent sightings beforehand (see useful contacts).

4. Dhiarizos Valley

The Dhiarizos Valley road is one of the most attractive routes for birdwatchers to follow when travelling from the south-west coast to the Troodos Mountains. Apart from the beauty of the scenery along the route the many and varied types of habitat which the road transects support a broad variety of species and there are many points along the way where one can safely stop to birdwatch.

The valley road is reached by turning right off the Limassol to Paphos road onto the F616 just south of the Asprokremnos Dam turn. After 2.5 km. the road forks with the left hand F617 branch also leading to Troodos (see footnote) but on a longer, more elevated route along the west ridge of the valley. However, for greater birdwatching variety, the valley bottom is usually the best route.

The F616 road initially passes through cereals and grasslands where Black Francolin call and Fan-tailed Warbler and Corn Bunting are numerous. At Agios Georgios stands of

Pied Kingfisher

poplar and eucalyptus dot the area, and olive groves are plentiful; just beyond, tamarisk grow by the river and these attract flycatchers and a variety of warblers during migration periods. Near the hamlet of Kidsi the road crosses the river and climbs sharply through orchards and vineyards to Kedhares, giving panoramic views across the valley. Here Griffon Vulture sometimes plane overhead (though their numbers seem to be in decline) and, with luck, Long-legged Buzzard may be seen. Agios Nikalaos is the next village of note and at this point the scenery changes to pine covered slopes and vine patterned hillsides where Bonelli's Eagle roam and Cretzschmar's Bunting breed. At Mandria the F616 joins the E802 Limassol – Troodos road and just beyond is the Kato (lower) Platres boundary. In spring the area throbs with the song of Nightingale, and the scarce and irregular Yellowhammer seems to favour this spot in winter.

The recommended route to Troodos from here is through Pano (upper) Platres – where refreshments and sundry facilities are available and where guide maps for local walks can be obtained from the tourist office – thence onwards via steep, climbing bends to intersect the main Limassol – Troodos (B8) road at a point opposite the Psilo Dendro trout farm and restaurant (see Map 8). Turn left here to travel a further 11.0 km. uphill to Troodos village, or, alternatively, cross the road to park near the restaurant if wishing to walk the Caledonian trail (see page x).

Note. The F617 route via Kholetria, Kelokedhara, Salamiou and Arminou reconnects with the F616 between Arminou and Kedhares. The route is longer but the chances of seeing Long-legged Buzzard are slightly enhanced. Perhaps travelling up to Troodos one way and back the other, if Long-legged Buzzard is not seen on the uphill journey, would be the answer for those keen to add this species to their list.

5. Paphos Airport road
2.8 km. from Asprokremnos Dam, heading towards Paphos, is a sign indicating Paphos International Airport 4.0 km. (E 603), the turning to the left is 500 m. ahead. The road to the airport passes through cultivated land where Calandra Lark and Black Francolin breed and often afford good views. Close to the airport the road passes a eucalyptus grove bordering the coastal strip and the area generally is good for passage migrants and winter visitors. Sea watching here in spring has produced some of the island's few Common Scoter sightings.

Warning
Airports can be sensitive areas – it is recommended you do not linger with optics on the perimeter.

6. Paphos headland (Map 4)
Return to the main Limassol – Paphos road from the airport and turn left. 300 m. further on is a right hand turn to Nata (F 622) which is the junction at which those returning from Asprokremnos Dam via the Kholetria to Phinikas route would rejoin the road.

5.5 km. beyond this junction, having passed through Achelia and Koloni, you come to Geroskipou, which merges almost imperceptibly with the outskirts of Paphos, and a further 2.0 km. ahead there is a 'Welcome to Paphos' sign. Just beyond this sign there is a major roundabout ❶ with roads off heading right towards the General Hospital and Polis, left to Kato (lower) Paphos and the tourist area, and straight ahead to Paphos town centre.

Two alternative routes may be followed from here to Paphos headland.

A. Going left at the roundabout follow the well-signposted route towards the port for a distance of 5.0 km. along the Leodores Denais and Poseidon roads. The port is predominated by a fort and the headland lies beyond. The headland is reached either by heading right up the unmade road ❷ just short of the port area, or by continuing towards the fort and turning right onto the adjacent unmade road ❸ leading to the coastal track. The headland has been fenced alongside this track but access to both the landward and seaward sides of the fence remain at present.

B. The alternative route is to continue towards Paphos town centre from the roundabout for a further 2.0 km. (Philips Hipermarket, 300 m. on the right beyond the roundabout is an excellent store for general provisions), passing through one set of traffic lights near to an impressive sculptured head of Archbishop Makarios and then filtering left at the next traffic lights. Follow this road through two more sets of traffic lights to turn right 500 m. beyond at the lighthouse sign ❹. Immediately on the right of this side road is the Apollo Tavern and behind it the Apollo Hotel ❺ where, during migration periods, a Cyprus Ornithological Society (1957) representative may be found beside the swimming pool from 10.30 am to 12.30 pm. Visitors are very welcome to call in to hear the latest birding news and to pass on their own sightings.

The lighthouse is clearly visible from here and may be reached via a rough stony road. Alternatively, for the less mobile, a smoother ride can be found by continuing south past the lighthouse turn to take the next turning right ❻ along Ayios Gelationis Street which leads on via a well graded track to the ruins of the Odeion which is next to the lighthouse.

The trees and bushes in this area ❼ often hold a variety of warblers whilst the open grassland between the lighthouse and the shore is much favoured by various races of Yellow Wagtail, wheatears, pipits, larks and buntings.

Offshore Cory's Shearwater may be seen mainly in April and May, and Yelkouan Shearwater randomly throughout the year. However sea watching is more likely to result

27

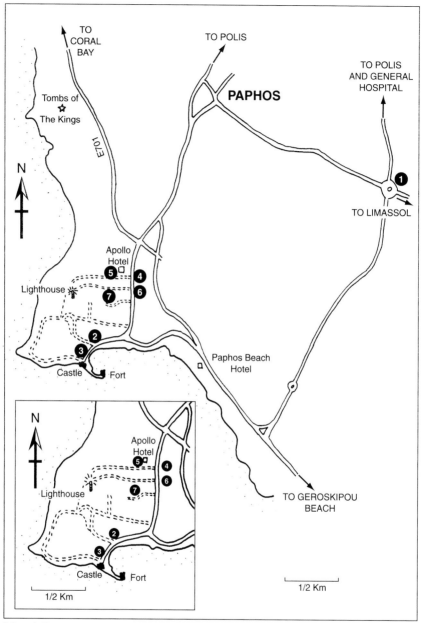

Map 4. Paphos headland.

in the first sight of large migrants making for land or, as frequently happens, egrets and herons coasting by. The best results are likely to be achieved by walking a circuit from the lighthouse which takes in the various habitats of the area, either early in the morning or late in the afternoon. Many rarities have been seen about the headland – Cream-coloured Courser, Little Swift, Hooded Wheatear and Pale Rock Sparrow for example – and repeat

28

visits can be rewarding. This second route to Paphos headland is the one recommended and directions to the following sites commence from Paphos Lighthouse.

West

1. Mavrokolymbos Dam, Ayios Yeoryios and Cape Drepanum (Map 5)

Leaving Paphos Lighthouse return to the road, turn left and left again at the first traffic lights onto the E701 Tombs of Kings road which leads direct to Ayios Yeoryios some 18.0 km. distant. After 9.7 km. a sign marks a right hand turn up a rough road to the

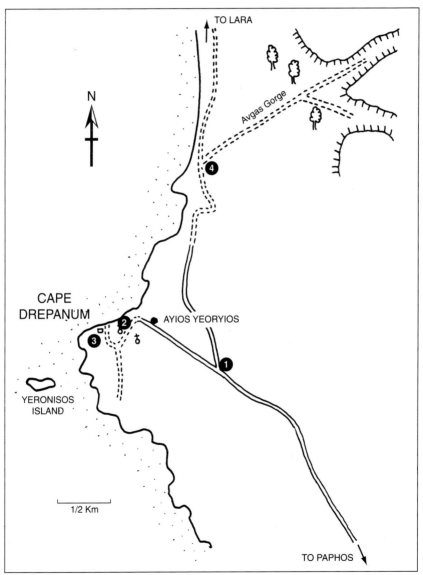

Map 5. Cape Drepanum and Avgas Gorge.

Mavrokolymbos Dam which lies 2.0 km. from the road in a defile beyond a banana plantation. In common with several of the dams in Cyprus the main water catchment area seems to offer a meagre attraction to anything other than winter wildfowl, but the fringes of the reservoir and points where shallow pools occur are always worth checking and have produced some excellent sightings.

Back on the main road and a little further on past Coral Bay the road diverges and from here it is the E714 that heads to Ayios Yeoryios. Entering Ayios Yeoryios the road to the Akamas peninsula is signposted to the right ❶ and via this road one can reach both the Avgas Gorge and Lara, descriptions of which follow.

To reach Cape Drepanum continue bearing left through Ayios Yeoryios, past, on the right, a large white church with a red roof ❷ and, on the left, a small old stone-built church outside of which is a rag-strewn bush. The downhill track at this point becomes rough but is passable to all vehicles and leads to the fishing shelter ❸ closeby the cape and overlooking Yeronisos Island.

Yeronisos Island hosts breeding Yellow-legged Gull and Rock Dove, and herons and egrets frequently rest here when on passage. The grassland of the cape, which is dotted with cistus, is extremely good for larks, wheatears, pipits and wagtails, and the bushes under the cave-lined cliffs behind the fishing shelter provide shelter and food for other passerines. From the clifftop near the red-roofed church it is worth scanning the sea for shearwaters.

2. Avgas gorge (Map 5)

2.0 km. to the north of Ayios Yeoryios the Avgas gorge is signposted to the right ❹. At the mouth of the gorge there are extensive citrus groves and, beyond, juniper covered slopes shelve towards the gorge bottom where there is a mix of vegetation, and a stream flows for much of the year. In winter the gorge attracts Wallcreeper, and in spring and autumn migrants shelter and feed here in profusion; resident species include Blue Rock Thrush.

This site should be covered on foot or by four-wheel drive vehicle.

3. Lara

Lara, some 5.0 km. beyond Avgas gorge, is the gateway to the wild and as yet unspoiled Akamas Peninsula. It is reached by a rough road best suited to four-wheel drive vehicles.

Unless exploring or venturing further into the Akamas hinterland the journey might disappoint those seeking to add to their list of species – in the main the south coast is more productive. However, for those making the journey, there is a welcoming elevated taverna at Lara which overlooks the sea and the beach and from here shearwaters, Audouin's Gull and Gull-billed Tern have been seen in recent times. The beach, which is fringed with tussock grass and bushes, is a favourite haunt of larks. wheatears and pipits, and Sardinian Warbler are to be found in the cistus behind the beach.

To the north beyond the bay overlooked by the taverna is a protected beach where, in summer, Green and Loggerhead Turtle come ashore to lay their eggs.

North West

Polis area

For the purpose of this guide the Polis area commences some 12.0 km. south of Polis and extends north-west along the coast beyond Polis to Cape Arnauti. For those with time to spare the area to the north-east along the coast and over the hills to Kato Pyrgos is also well worth a visit. It is extremely scenic and often good for raptors and passerines which transit the island via Cape Kormakiti. However it is unlikely to produce species different to those to be found at the sites detailed below. It should also be noted that the 'Green Line'- the border between the Greek Cypriot and Turkish Cypriot Republics – commences just beyond Kato Pyrgos and en route there are a number of UN posts. In the region of these posts optical aids should be used with discretion and cameras not at all!

East and south-east of Polis there are also a number of interesting roads and tracks which converge on Stavros – situated in the heart of the Paphos Forest – before they continue on into the Troodos mountains or head south in the direction of Paphos. Along these tracks both Goshawk and Bonelli's Eagle may be encountered but emphasis is on the word 'may'! A promising area close to Polis which is worth a diversion to search for these species is Stavros – tis – Psokas, a permanent Game Reserve situated in coniferous woodland which is well signposted to the east of Polis on the approach to the town. Until a few years ago Imperial Eagle was to be found here and locals claim there are still occasional sightings.

The area on which this guide concentrates has a variety of habitats which include an inland reservoir, a watercourse with dense reedbeds and the scenically beautiful Akamas Peninsula which is cultivated here and there but which predominately remains in its wild, undeveloped state, covered in Aleppo Pine, juniper and rock rose.

1. Paphos Forest

En route to the Polis area and East of the Paphos to Polis road there are many roads and tracks which criss cross the adjacent foothills and extend into Paphos Forest and beyond. They penetrate areas largely untouched by tourism, where life has a slower pace and the donkey remains a commonly used beast of burden. Chukar and Black Francolin call from the vine-covered slopes, Red-rumped Swallow breed in culverts beneath the roads and the harsh chatter of Great Spotted Cuckoo mingles with the song of Black-headed Bunting. On the woodland hills there might be a chance sighting of a Bonelli's Eagle or, in the forest regions, a Goshawk. A drive through these areas is highly recommended.

A good starting point is to be found 14.0 km. from Paphos on the B7 road to Polis at Stroumpi where the Cedar Valley route is signposted. A suggested short route drive is from here to Kannaviou and on to Pano Panayia before circling back to the B7 via Khrysorroyiatissa Monastery, Khoulou, Letinbou and Tsadha.

A short diversion off this route from Pano Panayia is recommended. Approaching Pano Panayia from the direction of Stroumpi the road rises through a series of bends, in the town itself turn sharp left down a narrow road signposted Cedar Valley and barely 2.0 km. down this road the Monashilakas picnic site is located and signposted on the right. The picnic area is large and there are many tables with their own designated barbecues. In the trees above the site you can find birds typical of the pine forests but the most interesting spot lies just below the picnic site where a track overlooks a small orchard and an open area with a small stream. Here Masked Shrike breed and Hawfinch may be seen into early spring when a wonderful bank of orchids may also be found here.

Recommended alternatives for those wishing to range further afield are from Kannaviou north along dirt tracks to the well signposted forestry station at Stavros, or through Cedar Valley from Pano Panayia to Troodos via historic Kykko Monastery and the mountain village of Pedhoulas: both are excellent birding routes.

A word of warning, ensure you start longer journeys with a full tank of fuel!

2. Evretou Dam (Map 6)

The dam is located approximately 26.0 km. from Paphos and 12.0 km. from Polis to the east of the main B7 Paphos to Polis road. The reservoir is crescent shaped and natural contours prevent the whole surface of the reservoir being viewed from any single easily accessible point but there is a road to the dam and a track from the south from which a check on the reservoir may be made in two bites.

Travelling from the direction of Paphos pass through Stroumpi and Giolou and 3.5 km. beyond Giolou turn right towards Simou on the E712 road. Continue up a steep incline for 1.0 km. before turning left ❶ onto a well-defined track at the head of which is a concrete water tank ❷. Turn left at the water tank, taking the upper of the two tracks which branch off here, and continue for 200 m. to a point where the track widens and it is possible to park ❸ and look northwards along the longest arm of the reservoir. The track to the east

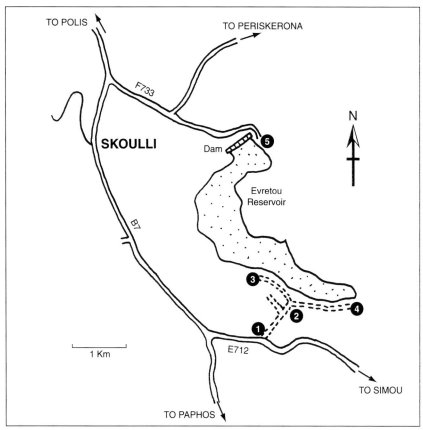

Map 6. Evretou Dam.

continues down a steep incline to where a feeder stream flows into the reservoir and where, in years of abundant rainfall, subsidiary pools form **4** and attract a variety of herons, egrets and waders. However, the reservoir site is best in late autumn, winter and early spring when substantial numbers of mixed wildfowl gather there. Recent records have included White-headed Duck and Red-crested Pochard.

The north to south arm of the reservoir can best be viewed from the dam itself **5** which may be reached by returning to the Paphos-Polis road, turning right and continuing for 3.0 km. to the village of Skoulli before turning right again on to the F733 Periskerona and Lysos road (marked Evretou Dam, just beyond the F733 sign); 1.8 km. along this road is a right hand fork which leads to the dam 1.0 km. ahead.

Like the south-east arm of the reservoir this area is also favoured by a variety of wildfowl in late autumn, winter and early spring. The dam itself straddles the Stavros-tis-Psokas river valley- a much used migrant flyway- and the conveniently provided seat by the side of the dam can prove to be a most productive resting point from which to birdwatch when passage is underway,

Note. On the right hand side of the road in Skoulli village, the Herpetological Society of Cyprus has an exhibition which shows all of the snakes, venomous and non-venomous, to be found on the island. The exhibition is open daily from 9.00 am to1.00 pm and again from 3.00 pm to 7.00 pm; entrance costs 50 cents per adult, children are admitted free.

3. Polis reedbeds (Map7)

From observations it is clear that the reed-shrouded river valley that enters Polis from the south is a major flyway for both passerine and non-passerine migrants.

In spring, when the reedbeds hold water, the area is a safe haven for a variety of species replenishing their body fat levels before making the sea crossing to Turkey or when held back by adverse weather conditions. At such times Common Bittern, Little Bittern, Night Heron and Purple Heron may be seen along with Sedge, Reed and Great Reed Warbler and, with luck, Penduline Tit as well; Savi's Warbler also frequent this stretch but they are more likely to be heard than seen. Overhead movements of raptors are random and variable, harriers, Goshawk, Eleonora's and Red-footed Falcon occur and Bonelli's Eagle, which is thought to be resident in the nearby area of Stavros-tis Psokas, are often seen here according to the locals.

The river valley is surrounded by olive and orange groves, by fields of wheat, barley and alfalfa and these combine to attract a very broad range of species. In consequence the area generally is a prime birding spot which can be reached most simply as follows:

32.0 km. from Paphos and 3.0 km. from Polis is a signpost to Chrysokhou (F750) to the west of the road. Take this road and drive to the village which is just ahead ignoring the diverging roads to the left; proceed through the village and bear right at the first turn ❶, passing a timber store on the left. The downhill track at this point becomes rough but improves after some 50 m. where it turns right onto a good, well-graded road which runs northward roughly parallel with the main road and terminates in Polis. This route is suitable for all vehicles and affords excellent views of the flyway along its length and has the added advantage of allowing frequent stops without inconvenience to other road users. For those with four-wheel drive vehicles an alternative route may be followed by continuing past the graded road turn for a further 100 m., crossing a river bridge ❷ then turning right and bearing right at the next fork ❸ in the road to follow the path of the river. This road, which is rough over much of its length, ends after 2.5 km. at Prodhromi (on the outskirts of Polis); there are junctions at 1.4 km. and 1.7 km. but these should be ignored. The benefit this road offers is its proximity to the river which enables checks to be made of the reedbeds along the route for acrocephalus warblers and skulking crake species.

Another excellent point for checking the reedbeds and their surrounds lies closer to Polis but is again suitable only for four-wheel drive vehicles or those who do not mind getting their feet wet. 500 m. from Polis, on the western side of the road, is a cluster of buildings ❹, one of which has a prominent Keo sign mounted on its side; between the buildings there is a rough road reducing to a track which, just past the end of the buildings, transects the graded road mentioned earlier. The track continues in a westerly direction towards a rubbish tip in which an abandoned vehicle, facing nose down, is clearly visible. In spring the area around the tip attracts large flocks of finches, especially Serin; ahead the river crosses a shallow ford which is a magnet to passing heron, egret, occasional duck and frequently Kingfisher. After a further 500 m. the track enters a clearing bordered by orange groves, eucalyptus trees and arable land. This is a favoured roosting site for many species as well as a gathering point for weather-held migrants waiting to go north. The area generally is particularly productive immediately post-dawn and pre-dusk.

4. Polis campsite (Map 7)

The campsite ❻ is situated within a substantial stand of eucalyptus trees adjacent to the shore and is clearly visible from Latsi beach. The site can be reached on foot along the beach or by vehicle via Polis town centre where it is clearly signposted ❺. Within the eastern edge of the campsite is a stream where Kingfisher may be found in spring, autumn and winter, and the woodland and its environs provide a refuge for many species when foul weather develops.

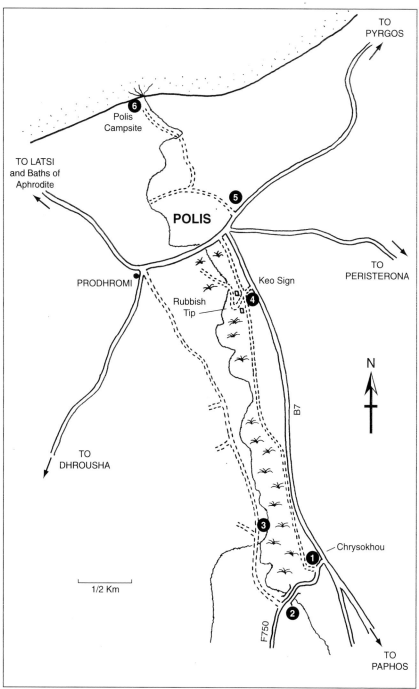

Map 7. Polis reedbed.

34

Purple Heron

The Akamas Peninsula

The north-west promontory of the island is known as the Akamas; the area largely remains wild, unspoilt and beautiful due in no small measure to the periodic use of part of it as a military training area and this has prevented encroachment by developers. In recent years some development has taken place on the eastern approach to the Akamas Peninsula, mainly between Polis and Latsi Port, and this is now creeping even further westward towards the legendary Baths of Aphrodite. Pleasure boats now ply the northern coast and commercial four-wheel drive safaris have also 'found' the Akamas. Despite these intrusions, and because of its relatively large size with poor quality dirt roads and tracks, the area remains a haven for birds and the birdwatcher who wishes to get away from it all.

The Akamas has a variety of habitats: the higher ground is liberally dotted with Aleppo Pine interspersed with juniper and Thorny Burnet bushes whilst at lower levels fig, carob and olive groves are numerous, often shielding fields of cereals from the wind . The north coast is predominately rocky and covered in scrub but the west coast has sandy beaches where Green and Loggerhead Turtles come ashore to lay their eggs.

This variety of habitats attract a broad range of species, especially during spring and autumn migration when the northward pointing finger of the Akamas Peninsula acts as a funnel for birds moving across the Mediterranean to and from Europe. From April to August summer breeding visitors such as Masked Shrike, Red-rumped Swallow, Cretzschmar's and Black-headed Bunting swell the ranks of resident species which include Black Francolin, Chukar, Fan-tailed and Cetti's Warbler; in autumn huge flocks of duck, heron and egret migrate across Khrysokhou Bay and in winter rafts of assorted duck gather there.

The Akamas is also the year-round home of Sardinian Warbler. Previously this species was a passage migrant and winter visitor but in recent years it has established itself as a breeding resident and is fast expanding its range both southwards and eastwards in the island.

As mentioned, many of the dirt roads and tracks which criss cross the Akamas are of poor and variable quality. Few are negotiable without four-wheel drive vehicles, and after winter storms even the most powerful off-road vehicles can find some routes extremely challenging. For those without suitable transport or who prefer to walk, the following sites and routes are recommended.

1. Baths of Aphrodite caravan site.

Two main roads serve the north-west of the island: one connects with Prodhromi, and the other with Polis. To reach the Baths of Aphrodite, whichever of these roads you take, turn left from the respective town and continue west along the coast road through Latsi (sometimes spelt and pronounced Latchi) onwards to where the tarmac ends. Here there is a car park and restaurant and close by are the Baths of Aphrodite and the caravan site. The distances from Prodhromi and Polis are approximately 8.0 km. and 10.0 km. respectively.

The caravan site is situated on a promontory which has steep sided cliffs which drop away to the sea and from which there are panoramic views of the coastline. The site is reached by continuing past the car park, along the start of the coastal path and branching right on to an obvious access track. The promontory has parkland habitat dotted with carob and olive trees and a number of lentisc bushes. The site is served with water and at its westward end there are goat sheds. The ready availability of food in various forms and a constant supply of water attracts a wide variety of species, it is also an excellent spot from which to watch the overhead movement of migrants making for Cape Arnauti during spring passage and for observing the sometimes massive movement of herons, egrets and wildfowl across Khrysokhou Bay in autumn. Breeding birds include Sardinian, Olivaceous and Cetti's Warbler.

This is an excellent site for those with limited mobility who would prefer to sit and watch migrants passing and it is made even more so by the fact that food and beverages are available in the restaurant opposite the car parking area nearby.

Between Latsi and the Baths of Aphrodite in spring watch out for Fan-tailed Warblers in the cereal fields adjacent to the road and for Roller, shrikes and Black-headed Bunting on the overhead wires. The general area is also good for Black Francolin all year round.

2. Coastal path

There is a path from the Baths of Aphrodite which follows the coast northwest to Cape Arnauti over a distance of some 8.0 km. The path is potentially navigable by four-wheel drive vehicles, however attempting to do so is not recommended since, for much of the first 2.5 km., it is narrow, undulating, has few points at which vehicles can pass, has a surface which is uneven, sometimes crumbles at the edges after rain and, in places, has steep unfenced drops on the seaward side!! However for the walker this section of the track is perfectly safe and is an excellent vantage point from which to look for shearwaters feeding in Khrysokhou Bay and for coasting Audouin's Gull and migrants in general.

After 2.5 km. the path descends to sea level and enters an open area which is sometimes cultivated and sometimes fallow. At this point the path forks with the left arm veering south towards the high ground. It is worth following the path for about 200 m. to a point where it starts to rise quite steeply. Here on both sides of the track there is running water which makes an ideal spot to take a refreshment break whilst watching birds coming to the water to drink and to bathe. During migration periods warblers, flycatchers, hirundines, bee-eaters and buntings are drawn here in substantial numbers and at other times resident finches abound.

From here return to the coastal path either by retracing your steps or, if the plain has been left fallow, by transecting it. During migration this area is often teeming with ground-feeding species and especially various races of Yellow Wagtail, Isabelline, Northern and Black-eared Wheatear, Short-toed and occasionally Calandra Lark, Cretzschmar's and Ortolan Bunting.

At the western end of the plain the track winds through juniper scrub, and about 1.0 km. further on reaches Fontana Amorosa, a minor promontory covered in scrub. The rocky

Plate 9. *Paphos lighthouse showing the dry stony area in the immediate vicinity, at times alive with larks, pipits, wagtails and buntings in spring.*   *Graham Hearl*

Plate 10. *Paphos headland showing the typical scrubby bushes which attract migrants on their first landfall.*   *Graham Hearl*

Plate 11. *Cape Drepanum with Yeronisos Iland in the background. This headland to the north of Paphos is a prime location for ground-feeding passerines and flocks of herons and egrets on passage.*

Arthur Stagg

Plate 12. *Evretou Dam, showing the northern arm of the reservoir, lies beneath a main migrant flyway and is especially good from late autumn to early spring for mixed flocks of wildfowl.*

Arthur Stagg

Plate 13. The caravan site at Baths of Aphrodite with Khrysokhou Bay beyond. A gathering point for outbound and inbound migrants and a superb location from which to watch passage movements.

Arthur Stagg

Plate 14. The Akamas Peninsula looking north-west along the north coast. The Akamas is the last staging post for migrants in spring and one of the first landfalls in autumn.

Graham Hearl

Plate 15. *Paphos Forest at Monashilakas picnic site: typical territory for Masked Shrike and Hawfinch.*
Graham Hearl

Plate 16. *Looking west from Cape Greco depicting the flat coastal terrain at the extreme south-east corner of the island: another very good migration spot but underwatched.*
Arthur Stagg

coast here is frequented by Kingfisher, and the promontory itself is often extremely good during migration for a variety of warblers, wheatears, shrikes, larks, Black-headed Bunting and Quail.

The distance from the western end of the Fontana Amorosa promontory to Cape Arnauti is approximately 2.0 km. and the track passes through a relatively barren area of alluvium rock before entering juniper scrub. Here, in cover, passage birds are often numerous and the area can be a hot-spot in April for the scarce and elusive Barred Warbler.

Cape Arnauti is relatively unprepossessing but it is an excellent site for weather-bound migrants and for watching their departure and arrival. The barren nature of the northern shoreline of the Akamas results in a paucity of waders of all kinds.

NB. As mentioned previously the Akamas is randomly used for military exercises. Prominent signs in Greek and English denote the areas used and red flags are flown whenever entry is prohibited.

The return journey from the Baths of Aphrodite to Cape Arnauti is approximately 16.0 km. and the risk of dehydration is high, especially in the warmer months, so ample water should be carried.

Because of the rough terrain in parts of the area coupled with its isolation it is recommended for safety reasons that visitors do not walk alone.

3. Smiyies track

Approximately 1.5 km. from Latsi, heading towards the Akamas Peninsula, there is a tee junction; the right hand turn leads to the Baths of Aphrodite whilst straight on, 2.0 km. ahead up a steep escarpment, lies the village of Neon Chorion. Drive through the village and you will join Smiyies Track. A further 2.0 km. along the track, through a miscellany of carob, olive and fig orchards, cultivated fields and Aleppo Pine woodland, stands the ancient church of Ayios Minas. 100 m. before the church, at the side of the track, a permanent spring provides a constant water trickle which draws a variety of birds to drink and bathe. Across the track in the shade of the trees is an excellent vantage point (particularly suitable for the less mobile) at which to linger and watch the activity. In April and May Red-rumped Swallow and House Martin collect mud from the trickle for nest building, and during migration, a constant stream of passage birds always seem to be present. Extreme island rarities such as River Warbler and Olive-tree Warbler have been recorded here.

About 200 m. before the Ayios Minas church there is a minor track which veers off left to the south-east and wends its way through open orchard and mixed deciduous woodland. In spring especially this is an excellent area in which to cast about, and although private land, the local landowners, at present, are amenable to visitors using the access. Golden Oriole seem to be particularly attracted to the area, Red-backed, Woodchat and Masked Shrike are abundant on passage as are Spotted, Pied and Collared Flycatcher (with a sprinkling of Semi-collared). From late April Black-headed Bunting sing from the tree tops and it is a favoured haunt of Great Spotted Cuckoo, probably attracted by the numerous resident Magpies which it parasitises. At dusk Scops and Little Owl, and maybe Long-eared Owl might be seen, along with hawking Nightjar.

500 m. beyond Ayios Minas church is the Smiyies picnic area and further on are trails which lead through the hills to the north and west coasts and across the spine of the Akamas to Dhrousha, and so on. Some of these tracks are occasionally graded and can appear to be suitable for non four-wheel drive vehicles but the earnest recommendation is not to proceed beyond the picnic site in anything other than a four-wheel drive vehicle!!

Other sites

1. Latsi beach

In spring when bad weather arrests the northward movement of birds the beach area on the western fringe of Latsi can hold large numbers of assorted wheatears, larks and pipits.

41

Central
Troodos Mountains area
The Troodos mountains are by no stretch of the imagination a birdwatchers haven – a far greater variety of birds is to be found in the lowlands – but it is the area within which endemic races of Wren, Coal Tit, Short-toed Treecreeper, Jay and Crossbill occur. There is also the faint chance – no more than that – of seeing Imperial Eagle.

Pano Platres, nestling amongst the hills at an elevation of 950 m. is the resort centre of the area. It has restaurants and hotels, banks and shops and also the local Tourist Information Bureau. The village of Troodos, some 450 m. higher, is less well endowed with general facilities but it comes into its own position of prominence when, in winter, snow falls and skiing commences.

In both Platres and Troodos, Pallid Swift, House and Crag Martin breed whilst in the surrounding woodlands Masked Shrike, Olivaceous Warbler and Cretzschmar's Bunting

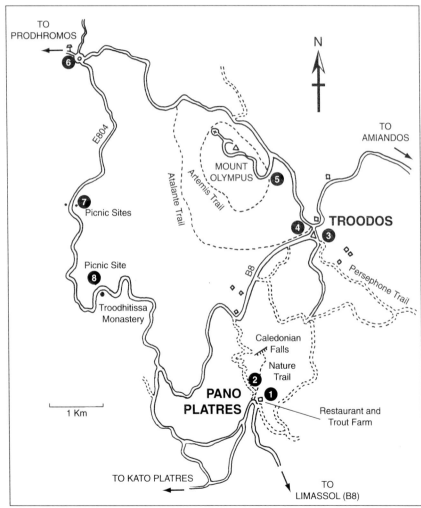

Map 8. Troodos trails.

42

are to be found in spring and summer alongside the endemic races of woodland birds previously mentioned.

Within the area generally there are numerous forest paths, or trails as they are called locally. Some are short, some long, some can be driven, some cannot. There is in fact something to suit most tastes and abilities and along these trails the chance of seeing all of the endemic sub-species is good.

A glance at a map will show a multitude of roads and tracks running in all directions to connect towns and villages located between the coast and the Troodos mountains. Some are easier to travel or are more scenic than others and for the first time visitor the choice can be confusing. Bearing in mind the aim of making the journey will be to maximise the time and opportunity to track down the endemic sub-species the two recommended routes covered below take that into consideration. One is a fast route from Limassol to Troodos via Garyllis Valley and the other, commencing on the Paphos to Limassol road, close to the Asprokremnos Dam site, also leads to Troodos but via a more meandering, scenic and potentially more bird-rich route which follows the Dhiarizos Valley.

1. Limassol to Troodos via Pano Platres
Connect with the B8 Limassol to Troodos road at a point approximately midway along the new Limassol bypass and drive north towards Khalassa. 3.5 km. from the junction on the left-hand side of the road, just beyond a small, red-roofed church, on the brow of a hill, is the Polemedhia Dam. This dam is well stocked with fish and has, in winter to early spring, sometimes attracted Pygmy Cormorant and Great Crested Grebe so it is worth scanning if time allows. 14.0 km. northward the Kouris Dam, the largest in Cyprus, can be seen away to the left, just short of Khalassa. The road continues on for 10.0 km. to Trimiklini then on for a further 12.0 km. through Moniatis to clip the northern edge of Pano Platres at a point adjacent to the Psilo Dendro trout farm and restaurant near to the point where the Caledonian Falls nature trail begins (see below); Troodos village lies 11.0 km. beyond this point.

Alternatively, just beyond Trimiklini, a most pleasant alternative route can be taken by turning left and travelling via Periphedi and Mandria (where it joins the Dhiarizos Valley route) and on into the village of Pano Platres. The B8 Limassol to Troodos road may be rejoined by driving on through the village of Platres.

2. Dhiarizos Valley
This route is covered in detail under South-west Paphos area No. 4 as the main birding areas are in the lower reaches of the valley which can be covered in part of a day when included with a visit to Asprokremnos Dam.

Platres and Troodos paths and trails (Map 8)
Platres
1. Caledonian Falls nature trail
As previously mentioned this trail starts on the northern outskirts of Pano Platres at a point where the B8 Limassol to Troodos road passes the Psilo Dendro trout farm and restaurant access ➊. The nature trail is not to be confused with the adjacent Caledonian trail which is a wide track that is passable to vehicles and which connects with the B8 road 3.0 km. south of Troodos. The nature trail commences by the left side of the Restaurant following the wide track until the first bend ➋ where the nature trail continues straight on and meanders through a heavily wooded area following the course of a stream to finally reach the waterfall 1.0 km. from the starting point. A reasonable degree of fitness is required to negotiate some of the stretches of the walk where it crosses back and forth across the stream, especially where it nears the falls and when the stream is in flood, but no more than that. It is a delightful walk at anytime of the year and hosts one of the largest concentrations of Wren to be found anywhere in the mountains. Other endemic sub-species feature here too but are more often heard than seen. It is possible to connect with

43

the Caledonian trail by continuing uphill past the falls, but returning back along the nature trail is the more scenic and pleasant option.

Troodos

Three trails start from or near Troodos and interconnect with others which extend like tendrils through the mountains. They trace their way through forest comprised mainly of Troodos Pine but with occasional glimpses of the lovely endemic Golden Oak.

1. Persephone trail

To reach this trail turn right off the B8 at the southern end of Troodos village, past the Troodos Hotel and follow the signs pointing towards the Police Station and the Civic restaurant. 200 m. along this road, on the left, is an unmade road leading downhill which passes a trail guide painted on a wood block mounted in a shelter ❸. This is the Persephone trail but confusingly the trail guide is titled 'Pouziouris' Nature Trail. It would seem that this is a collective name for a multitude of trails depicted on the painted guide board.

The Persephone trail is broad and well graded and may be walked or driven. After nearly 2.0 km. it gives elevated distant views of Amiandos Dam and shortly after there are branch tracks leading to Vrysos, Kryos Potamas, Psilon Dendron and Poyziaris.

Most of the endemic sub-species can be seen along the first 1.0 km. of track. Experience suggests that a sit and wait approach from a good viewpoint usually produces better and quicker results than pounding the trail.

2. Atalante trail

This trail begins at the northern end of Troodos village, opposite the main car parking area ❹. The trail is 9.0 km. in length and terminates on the road between Troodos and Prodhromas. It is unlikely to yield anything more than the Persephone trail.

3. Artemis trail

This trail is reached by leaving the northern end of Troodos village, driving towards Prodhromos and turning left onto the road signposted Mount Olympus. The trail ❺ completes a 7.0 km. circuit of Mount Olympus which at 1620 m. is the highest point in Cyprus. Chances of seeing Imperial Eagle are probably greatest from this trail and from the viewpoint adjacent to the radar station at the summit.

4. Other sites

Returning to Limassol via Prodhromos take the E804 road signposted at the Prodhromos roundabout ❻. 4.0 km. from the roundabout, on both sides of the road, are large, dispersed picnic areas within the forest which are equipped with tables, benches, barbecue points and rather rudimentary toilet facilities ❼. At weekends in summer this area – like most of the public picnic spots – tends to be crowded but during weekdays it is an excellent site at which to look for the endemic sub-species plus Masked Shrike, Hoopoe and Olivaceous Warbler in season.

3.5 km. further on towards Limassol, next to Troodhitissa Monastery, is another attractive picnic area ❽ with a stream running through it. The additional species often encountered here is Grey Wagtail.

For visitors spending a few days in the mountains there are many points of scenic beauty and birdwatching interest to be found by following a circuit taking in Troodos – Kyperounta – Kakopetria – Pedhoulas – Troodos.

East

Larnaca area (Map 9)

Larnaca is the largest town on the south-east coast of Cyprus. It is served by an International airport, has good quality roads linking it to all other major towns on the island and offers a broad spectrum of accommodation for visitors.

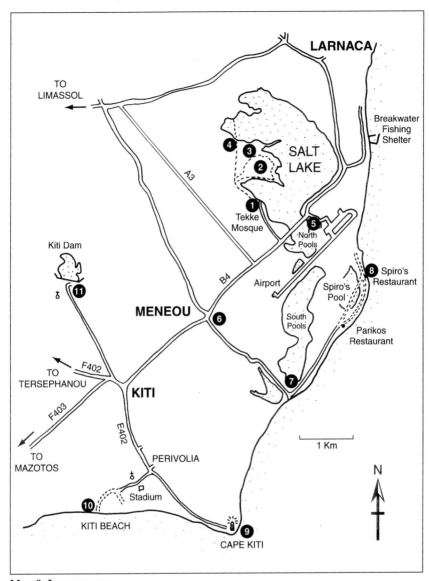

Map 9. Larnaca area.

Larnaca's attraction to birdwatchers is seasonal. Its main features are the salt lake, situated on the south-western edge of the town, supplemented by pools on both north and south sides of the airport. Cape Kiti, to the south of the town, is a good point from which to observe seasonal movements and, inland, Kiti Dam frequently attracts interesting species. Between the town and Cape Kiti are a number of gull gathering points and these, especially the one near to the Larnaca fishing shelter, are particularly good in winter.

The area is best visited in spring, autumn, and winter when the salt lake and the various nearby pools hold water; at these times the wetlands act as a veritable magnet to migrants and over-wintering species. In winters of severe weather in Euro-Asia rarities such as

45

Mute and Whooper Swan come south, with larger than usual flocks of assorted wildfowl, to take up temporary residence in the area. At such times here birdwatching can be exhilarating.

Despite a general scarcity of birds in the summer all is not lost for those who find themselves in the south-eastern sector of Cyprus before autumn migration commences, or before the wetlands in the immediate vicinity of Larnaca have been replenished by the first rains: Akhna Dam, some 20.0 km. north-east of the town, is an excellent year-round birdwatching haunt and should provide much to command interest even during the driest months (see page 48).

1. Larnaca Salt Lake
The main body of the lake lies between the town and the airport and is skirted by a major road which links Larnaca with Limassol and Nicosia. The lake is approximately half the size of the Akrotiri Salt Lake and is generally more accessible both by vehicle and on foot. In winter it hosts varying numbers of Greater Flamingo – 4,000 to 7,000 are not uncommon – and better views of these are usually obtained here than at Akrotiri due to the smaller size of the lake. Winter also provides a chance of seeing Great Crested and Black-necked Grebe, Pygmy Cormorant, White-fronted Goose, Ruddy Shelduck, Red-crested Pochard and sundry other wildfowl; the lake is also favoured by Mediterranean and Little Gull which visit randomly during the winter months. In spring a few lingering Greater Flamingo remain and Spoonbill are occasionally seen whilst Night Heron, Squacco Heron, Little Egret and Glossy Ibis are regular on passage. Generally the lake does not attract a wide variety of waders though Kentish Plover breed here and scarce migrants such as Avocet and Sanderling feature regularly. Caspian Tern has been recorded and Whiskered Tern pass annually. In the scrub surrounding the lake Spectacled Warbler breed and may be seen the year round; further back, in the cultivated fields, Calandra Lark breed but mainly disperse once their young have fledged. In late summer/early autumn the lake is usually dry and there is little to attract wetland species.

The proximity of the lake to the airport, which is well signposted, makes it easy to find irrespective of the direction from which Larnaca is approached. An ideal viewpoint of the lake is from the general area of the historic Tekke Mosque ❶ which lies on the western fringe of the lake; this is clearly marked and is reached by turning north off the road which passes the airport. The Tekke has parking, restaurant and toilet facilities and is set amidst trees and gardens which attract a variety of passerines during the spring and autumn migration periods.

Closer approach to the western shores of the lake may be made along the tracks shown on the map ❷ ❸ & ❹ but caution is urged: the state of the tracks can vary with weather conditions.

2. Larnaca Airport pools (north)
Although originally part of the Larnaca Salt Lake these pools are now separated from the main body of the lake by the B4 road which runs from Larnaca to the airport and thence onward in a south-westerly direction towards Menou and Kiti. The pools are seasonal, their size and duration being dependent on the amount of winter rain. When active they may be viewed from the side of the road ❺ but those observers using cars should ensure they park only in authorised pull-off points. Despite the proximity to the airport and the busy road the pools have in the past attracted Mute and Whooper Swan, Shelduck and Gadwall in winter; both Little and Mediterranean Gull in winter and spring, and during the spring months a range of waders which has included Marsh and Terek Sandpiper, Avocet and Curlew; occasionally Whiskered Tern also occur.

3. Larnaca Airport pools (south)
From the northern pools continue south-west along the B4 road towards Menou and Kiti; the A3 Limassol road intersects the B4 1.2 km. before Menou. In Menou turn left where

the beach is signposted **6**; this road, which bisects the southern extension of the Larnaca Salt Lake, interconnects with another road, 2.6 km. ahead **7**, which follows the coast. In years of little rain these pools rapidly dry up and are largely devoid of birds, but when wet they have, in winter, attracted White-fronted Goose, Shelduck, Red-crested Pochard, and Lapwing together with Curlew, Marsh Sandpiper and Little Gull in spring.

4. Spiro's pool

Spiro's Pool is reached by turning left **7** where the road bisecting Larnaca Airport pools (south) intersects with the beach road, and by then following that road northwards. The road divides at Parikos restaurant with the right fork following the coastline and the left fork taking an alternative route through scrub before again connecting with the coastal track at a point near to Spiro's beach restaurant **8**. The scrub which the latter track cuts through is attractive to Spectacled Warbler.

Like other pools around the Larnaca Salt Lake Spiro's Pool is seasonal. In the past it has produced Red-breasted and White-fronted Goose, Ruddy Shelduck and Avocet, and Black-winged Pratincole in winter and Greater Sandplover and Black-tailed Godwit in spring.

The track may be followed beyond the pool, via the beach, as far as the airport boundary fence. In spring the cereal fields here are a breeding site for Calandra Lark, and they are a much favoured haunt of passing harrier species. Return via the same route.

5. Kiti lighthouse and beach

Cape Kiti is reached by bearing left in the town of Kiti onto the E402 road which passes through Perivolia. In Perivolia there is a tee junction; the left turn leads to the lighthouse area where building development is rapidly absorbing land once good for migrant passerines but even so the lighthouse **9** itself remains an excellent spot from which to observe general movements and to sea-watch for scarce passage migrants such as Arctic Skua. Alternatively take the right turn from Perivolia and proceed past the church on the right and the stadium on the left to join a road which intersects with another 700 m. further on. Turn right here and then almost immediately left, past a line of eucalyptus, and along an unmade track for 600 m. to reach the shore where there is a park bench type seat **10** from which you can seawatch in comfort. The scrubby shoreline is much favoured by wheatears, pipits and larks – and as yet there is no development on this site. A beach walk west from here towards Mazotos can be very productive when migration is underway: Hooded Wheatear has been seen in this general area.

6. Kiti Dam

Kiti Dam is 3.0 km. from Kiti and is reached by turning north-west in the town on to the F403 Mazotos and Alaminnos road; 500 m. down this road Teresfanou (F402) and Kiti Dam are signposted to the right. Turn here and after only 30 m. turn right again and after another 400 m., just past the Pimloss bakery, turn right once more and continue straight ahead to the dam which is some 2.0 km. distant. Continue past the small church which lies to the left of the track near the dam and bear right to park by eucalyptus and wattle trees at the foot of the wall of the dam **11**.

This is yet another site which can be excellent when the dam holds water but it often dries up completely in summer and even earlier in years of little rainfall. In winter it has produced White-fronted Goose, White-headed Duck, Red-crested Pochard, Water Rail and Moustached Warbler; in spring, egrets, Glossy Ibis, Spoonbill and Black-tailed Godwit have been recorded and if water remains into early summer then Black-winged Stilt, Spur-winged Plover and Little Ringed Plover are likely to breed.

Irrespective of the water level of the dam the trees and bushes near the recommended parking point often hold many migrant passerines.

Akhna and Cape Greco areas

Just over 45.0 km. east of Larnaca is Cape Greco, the easternmost point on the southern coast of the island. Approximately 16.0 km. north, in the direction of Famagusta, near Dherinia, the boundary between the Greek Cypriot and Turkish Cypriot enclaves begins and runs west past Akhna which is some 20.0 km. north-east of Larnaca. Within this loosely defined, largely flat peninsula much of the hinterland is given over to farming whilst the littoral (virgin not so many years since) is fast being developed to cater for the needs of a burgeoning tourist industry.

The area lies beneath a particularly active migration route used by birds moving between Africa and Euro-Asia. The busy nature of this route is exemplified by the fact that, until a few years ago, it was the heartland of a large migratory bird harvesting industry (for an industry it certainly was) centred on Paralimni that killed millions of birds by the use of limesticks and nets. Although now illegal here and throughout the island it is a practice which continues surreptitiously on a much smaller scale.

Perhaps the distance from Cape Greco and its environs from other notable birding locations on the island – made more so since partition – has caused the area to be largely overlooked these days by the main body of visiting birdwatchers. However it is an area that has much to offer and merits coverage especially during the migration seasons and in winter.

1. Akhna Dam (Map 10)

The dam is located to the south of the Akhna bypass road and can be reached from Larnaca by driving north-east on the B3 road towards Dhekelia for 10.5 km. to connect with the E303 road to Famagusta. 9.0 km. along this road a UN site with watchtower overlooking the 'Green Line' is signed 'Fort Bravo' ❶ ; 2.7 km. beyond this point the road is flanked by a crash barrier and dips as it crosses a river bed heavily overgrown with tamarisk on its southern side; on a rise to the left of the road is a stand of eucalyptus. This is the north-west extremity of Akhna Dam and the track ❷ leading south from the east bank of the river bed is an optional route to take on foot to reconnoitre the dam and its environs. However, approximately 1.0 km. beyond this point there is a turning right ❸ marked 'Akna Dam' which leads to the head of the dam, passing several pull-off points en route which connect with tracks around the dam. Beyond the wall of the dam there is a further extensive parking area ❹ from where the dam area may be explored.

Akhna Dam is what might be termed a birding hotspot. It offers excellent birdwatching throughout the year and regular observers here have recorded 14 species of wildfowl, 18 raptor, 30 wader and 15 warbler species. Highlights have included Dalmatian Pelican, Lanner Falcon, White-tailed Plover, Great Black-headed Gull and Dusky Thrush. In spring Little and Baillon's Crake and Great Snipe may be found; in summer there are resident breeding species such as Spur-winged Plover, Stone Curlew and Spectacled Warbler whilst in autumn southward movements often bring White and Black Stork, White Pelican and Spoonbill. Winter birding at Akhna is likewise excellent; Pygmy Cormorant, White-fronted Goose, Short-toed Eagle, Jack Snipe, Pied Kingfisher, Bluethroat in substantial numbers and Penduline Tit have all featured in recent records.

Akhna village abuts the border between the Greek Cypriot and Turkish Cypriot controlled areas of the island and in consequence there are military camps and UN checkpoints in the vicinity of the dam. The use of cameras and optics in general in areas overlooked by military personnel would be unwise but so far this has proved no problem to regular observers acting with discretion when birdwatching around the dam.

If leaving the dam to head onwards towards Paralimni and Cape Greco continue in a southerly direction past the parking area adjacent to the wall of the dam, turn left at the first junction on to the E304 road which leads to Avgorou. In Avgorou turn right then left to Leopetria to join the E305 road to Paralimni.

2. Paralimni Lake

Paralimni Lake, which is seasonal, (and is clearly visible on the western fringe of the town), has no particular or specific attractions. However Spotted Crake has occurred and

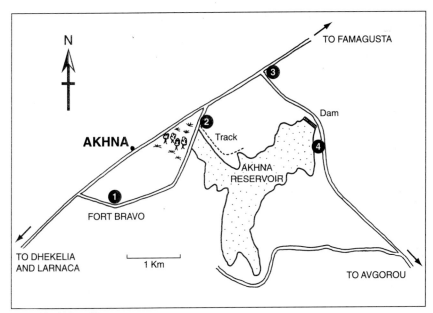

Map 10. Akhna Dam.

Caspian Plover was once claimed in spring and therefore it is a site worth checking if you are in the area.

3. Cape Greco (Map11)

There are two approaches to the cape: one from the northward Protaras side via the E307 road and the other from the west on the E306 road from Ayia Napa. The turnings on to the cape are signposted Kavo Gkreko and these access roads converge at a point ❶ overlooking the cape. Much of Cape Greco is given over to a communications site from which the public is denied entry though the abutting area to the north is open and accessible to vehicles.

Perhaps the best point from which to view the general area of the cape is from a craggy clifftop lookout which lies just to the west. The route to this lookout is signposted on the north-east flank approached via the Ayia Napa to Greco access road. The sign indicates a parking area, a nature trail and a viewpoint and although the track ❷ leading to the parking area ❸ is rough it is nevertheless passable to all vehicles. The clifftop viewpoint ❹ has a scattering of park-bench type seats from which the sea and the somewhat barren juniper scrub-dotted peninsula can be scanned.

In winter, in this general area, Great Black-headed and Audouin's Gull have been seen, and Finsch's Wheatear and Blue Rock Thrush are regular visitors. Offshore in spring shearwaters feed and herons and egrets coast north-east towards Syria and Turkey, whilst overhead, Osprey, harriers, falcons and hawks pass randomly (look out for Levant Sparrowhawk).

Around the cliffs the juniper scrub attracts large numbers of grounded migrants, especially larks, pipits, three races of Yellow Wagtail, four species of wheatear plus Crezschmar's and Ortolan Bunting. The autumn passage is equally rich and varied but separating some species in post-breeding or juvenile plumages can prove challenging.

For the venturesome – preferably with a four-wheel drive vehicle – a rough subsidiary track may be reached by turning right 500 m. after entering the Ayia Napa road access to the cape at a point marked simply 'path' ❺. This track gives access to the beach and to

49

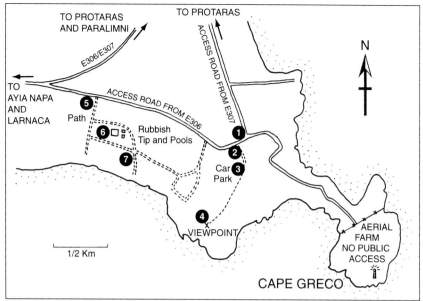

Map 11. Cape Greco.

the west flank of the elevated viewpoint. In addition the left hand fork, where the track branches, leads to a rubbish tip and two adjacent malodorous, oozy pools ❻ which despite their uncongenial nature, attract a variety of birds. The track continues eastwards past the tip to connect with another track on the right ❼ leading to the shore.

Other flora and fauna of Cyprus

Flora

Cyprus is one of the treasure-houses of the Mediterranean for plants and wild flowers. There are approximately 1,820 species on the island of which 121 are endemics. 47 species and sub-species of orchid are to be found and identification of the latter offers a real challenge to the amateur botanist.

The most important region is the Troodos mountain range which hosts 44 local endemics plus another 36 of the island endemics. This area is followed in importance by the Pendadahtilos Range with Kyrenia and Kythrea, in the Turkish enclave, which has15 local endemics plus another 35 island endemics. Third in botanical importance is the Akamas Peninsula with 1 local endemic and 28 island endemics, and it is in these two mountain regions and the Akamas Peninsula that most of the rare plants are to be found. Both the Troodos Mountains and the Akamas Peninsula are covered as prime birding spots in this book so for observers with an interest in both flowers and birds Cyprus makes for the perfect location, and the perfect companion guide is 'Wild Flowers of Cyprus' by George Sfikas.

Fauna

Cyprus is an extremely ancient island which has lacked a landbridge with Euro-Asia since early in the formation of the Mediterranean Sea. This consequent long – term isolation has probably caused the relative paucity of fauna to be found there – that is in comparison with the nearby mainland areas of the region. Even so there are 26 species of reptiles and amphibians plus 197 species of fish together with crabs, sponges and the like.

The small number of land mammals include Fox, Hare, mice and bats but most significant amongst these is the Mouflon, a long – horned wild sheep which, though rare, is still to be found in some of the more remote areas.

Reptiles include two of the world's seven species of sea turtle, Green and Loggerhead Turtle, both of which breed sparingly.

Amongst other reptiles are the Blunt-nosed Viper and Large Whip Snake (mentioned in the introduction to this book) together with the Montpelier Snake and Cat Snake both venomous but back-fanged and therefore not dangerous to humans unless handled carelessly; Cyprus Whip Snake, recorded only in the Troodos mountains; Coin Snake, Worm Snake and Grass Snake, the last was thought to be extinct on the island but was rediscovered a few years ago and is the most endangered on the island.

Lizards abound too, as might be expected on a warm Mediterranean island, and include geckos, sand lizards, agamids, chameleon and one ultra-rare skink, so far found only on the Akamas.

Butterflies and moths are likewise plentiful and can be seen in all months of the year.

Books covering these taxa occurring on Cyprus are hard to find but those with general or specific natural history interests, who visit the island, may find the books listed under 'Recommended books' helpful to them.

References

Cyprus Ornithological Society (1957) Annual reports 1992 to 1996
Cyprus Ornithological Society (1957) Monthly Newsletters 1992 to 1997
Flint P. R. & Stewart P. F. The Birds of Cyprus B.O.U. Check-list No. 6. (second edition) 1992.
RAFOS Expedition Reports, spring 1972, 1973, 1995 & 1997 (in prep.)

Recommended books

Jonsson L. Birds of Europe with North Africa and the Middle East, Chrisopher Helm 1992.
Sfikas G. Wild flowers of Cyprus, Efstathiadis Group, Attikis 1994.
Blamey M. & Grey-Wilson C. Mediterranean Wild Flowers, Harper Collins 1993.
Higgins L. G. & Hargreaves B. The Butterflies of Britain and Europe, Collins, London 1993.

Systematic Synopsis of Cyprus Records

Diver sp. *Gavia sp*
Accidental. One record only: an unidentified species of diver was seen offshore the Paphos Lighthouse area in May 1996.

Little Grebe *Tachybaptus ruficollis*
Winter visitor, passage migrant, occasionally remaining to breed when conditions permit. In recent years has been recorded in every month of the year.

Great Crested Grebe *Podiceps cristatus*
Winter visitor, passage migrant, has bred. Usually arrives in November and departs April to May.

Red-necked Grebe *Podiceps grisegena*
Accidental. Five records since 1981; mainly November/December but one in September.

Slavonian Grebe *Podiceps auritus*
Accidental. Two confirmed records, the last in March 1968.

Black-necked Grebe *Podiceps nigricollis*
Winter visitor. Occasionally remaining to breed. Usually arrives September to October and departs in April.

Cory's Shearwater *Calonectris diomedea*
Passage migrant. Passes March to May.

Mediterranean Shearwater *Puffinus yelkouan*
Passage migrant. Passes March to May.

Storm Petrel *Hydrobates pelagicus*
Accidental. Two confirmed records, the last in July 1956; plus a probable seen off Cape Andreas in April 1973.

Gannet *Morus bassanus*
Rare and irregular. Probably overlooked; most sightings have occurred in winter/early spring.

Cormorant *Phalacrocorax carbo sinensis*
Winter visitor, passage migrant. Has been recorded in all months except June and July.

Shag *Phalacrocorax aristotelis desmaresti*
Resident. Colonial breeder on cliffs and offshore islands.

Pygmy Cormorant *Phalacrocorax pygmeus*
Regular but random visitor in small numbers between August and May.

White Pelican *Pelecanus onocratalus*
Scarce passage migrant. Mainly passes in autumn but sometimes in winter and in spring.

Dalmatian Pelican *Pelecanus crispus*
Scarce and irregular passage migrant in spring and autumn.

Bittern *Botaurus stellaris*
Winter visitor and passage migrant. present from September to May.

Little Bittern *Ixobrychus minutus*
Passage migrant, has possibly bred. Passes April to May and in lesser numbers August to October.

Night Heron *Nycticorax nycticorax*
Passage migrant, has bred. Passes March to May and August to early October.

Squacco Heron *Ardeola ralloides*
Common passage migrant. From mid March, numerous April to May, returns mainly August to September, sometimes over-summering.

Cattle Egret *Bubulcus ibis*
Passage migrant in small numbers. Passes late March to May, and August to September. Has been recorded in all months except October.

Little Egret *Egretta garzetta*
Common passage migrant, sometimes summering and breeding, also a winter visitor. Passes March to May and August to October.

Great White Egret *Egretta alba*
Scarce passage migrant and winter visitor. Has been recorded all months except July.

Grey Heron *Ardea cinerea*
Common passage migrant and winter visitor in lesser numbers. Has been rcorded in all months of the year.Nest building recorded but no positive proof of breeding. Passes mainly March to May and August to October.

Purple Heron *Ardea purpurea*
Common passage migrant with largest numbers in autumn. Has summered. Passes mainly late March to May and August to September.

Black Stork *Ciconia nigra*
Very scarce passage migrant passing April to May and September to November. There have been random winter sightings.

White Stork *Ciconia ciconia*
Passage migrant in variable numbers though usually scarce. Passes March to May and August to October. Has summered and there are a few winter records.

Glossy Ibis *Plegadis falcinellus*
Common passage migrant in spring, considerably less common in autumn. Passes mainly late March to early May sometimes lingering for many weeks when conditions are favourable, and even summering. Returns mainly August to September.

Spoonbill *Platalea leucorodia*
Scarce passage migrant. Passes March to May, and September to October. There are random winter records.

Greater Flamingo *Phoenicopterus ruber*
Passage migrant and common winter visitor to Akrotiri and Larnaca Salt Lakes with flocks occasionally congregating on the sea. Mainly arriving October and departing March but non-breeding birds occasionally summer.

Mute Swan *Cygnus olor*
Has become a scarce but regular winter visitor in recent years, usually seen November to March.

Whooper Swan *Cygnus cygnus*
Accidental in winter. Only two accepted records in recent years in December January but others claimed.

White-fronted Goose *Anser albifrons*
Scarce winter visitor in variable numbers. Usually present November to February, but has been recorded in May.

Greylag Goose *Anser anser*
Scarce but fairly regular winter visitor in recent years. Recorded between November to February.

Red-breasted Goose *Branta ruficollis*
Accidental. Three winter records only.

Egyptian Goose *Alopochen aegyptiacus*
Accidental. Only three winter records since the 1950's, the last in 1989.

Ruddy Shelduck *Tadorna ferruginea*
Scarce winter visitor usually seen between December and March but once May and once September.

Shelduck *Tadorna tadorna*
Winter visitor and passage migrant, seen October to April.

Wigeon *Anas penelope*
Common autumn passage migrant and winter visitor with main movements occurring from late August to April.

Gadwall *Anas strepera*
A relatively scarce passage migrant and winter visitor, occurring September to April.

Teal *Anas crecca*
Passage migrant and very common winter visitor. Recorded in all months except July.

Mallard *Anas platyrhynchos*
Common winter visitor and passage migrant, becoming established as a breeding species at some dam sites.

Pintail *Anas acuta*
Very common winter visitor and passage migrant. Has been recorded in all months except July.

Garganey *Anas querquedula*
Common passage migrant, occasionally stays to breed. Passes mainly March to April, and August to September. Has been recorded in all months except December.

Shoveler *Anas clypeata*
Passage migrant and common winter visitor. Formerly bred but no recent records. Most years seen from August to April.

Marbled Duck *Marmaronetta angustirostris*
In the last century and earlier this century was a regular spring and summer visitor which sometimes bred. There are only four records in recent years of this species which is declining in number throughout its range. The last sighting was in 1992

Red-crested Pochard *Netta rufina*
Scarce but regular winter visitor, usually occurring between November and January.

Pochard *Aythya ferina*
Common winter visitor in variable numbers coupled with some movement through the island. Occurring mainly September to April usually peaking in January, has been recorded in every month of the year.

Ferruginous Duck *Aythya nyroca*
Scarce passage migrant and winter visitor. Has been recorded in every month of the year but there is no firm evidence of breeding.

Tufted Duck *Aythya fuligula*
Scarce winter visitor, usually from November to March, but occasionally into April. Some movement through the island.

Scaup *Aythya marila*
Accidental winter visitor. Last seen 1993; only five recent records.

Common Scoter *Melanitta nigra*
Accidental. Last positive identification was in 1957.

Goldeneye *Bucephala clangula*
Accidental. Last seen in the winter of 1991/2.

Smew *Mergellus albellus*
Accidental. Four winter records the last in 1985.

Red-breasted Merganser *Mergus serrator*
Scarce winter visitor, usually occurring from November to March and rarely into April.

Goosander *Mergus merganser*
Accidental. Only four records the last one in December 1977.

White-headed Duck *Oxyura leucocephala*
Scarce winter visitor from December to February. Previously a passage migrant.

Honey Buzzard *Pernis apivorus*
Passage migrant in spring and autumn, with heaviest passage in autumn. Passes mainly April to May, and August to October.

Black Kite *Milvus migrans*
Passage migrant passing mainly April to May, and August to September but stragglers have occurred through to December.

Red Kite *Milvus milvus*
Accidental. Two records only, the last in 1986. NB. The lineatus and aegyptius races of Black Kite have wing and tail features similar to Red Kite.

White-tailed Eagle *Haliaeetus albicilla*
Accidental. Six records, the last in 1968.

Lammergeier *Gypaetus barbatus aureus*
Accidental. Four records, the last in 1982.

Egyptian Vulture *Neophron percnopterus*
Scarce and irregular passage migrant. Last accepted sighting was in September 1996.

Griffon Vulture *Gyps fulvus*
Breeding resident often supplemented by winter influx, presumed to come from Turkey. There are indications of decline in the breeding population in some areas.

Black Vulture *Aegypius monachus*
Once a fairly common resident breeder; numbers have declined this century, the last reliable record was in 1982.

Short-toed Eagle *Circaetus gallicus*
Scarce passage migrant passing mainly April to July, and September to October, but has been recorded as early as March and as late as November.

Marsh Harrier *Circus aeruginosus*
Passage migrant and winter visitor, some non-breeding birds over-summer. Passes mainly March to May, and September to October.

Hen Harrier *Circus cyaneus*
Passage migrant and winter visitor with predominance of sightings in winter. Passes mainly March to May, and September to October but has been recorded in all months except June and July.

Pallid Harrier *Circus macrourus*
Passage migrant sometimes lingering into winter.Passes March to April, and September to October but has been recorded in all months except July.

Pallid Harrier

Montagu's Harrier *Circus pygargus*
Passage migrant, much less numerous than Pallid Harrier. Passes mainly March to May, and late August to October.

Goshawk *Accipiter gentillis*
Status uncertain but is thought to breed in small numbers in the Paphos Forest region.

Sparrowhawk *Accipiter nisus*
Passage migrant, winter visitor and occasional breeding. Occurs mainly September to May. Passes April to May, and September to October but spring passage is more pronounced. A pair bred in Paphos Forest in 1996.

Levant Sparrowhawk *Accipiter brevipes*
Scarce and irregular passage migrant. Most confirmed sightings have occurred April to May, and September to October.

Common Buzzard *Buteo buteo*
Common passage migrant and winter visitor. Passes mainly April to May,and September to October, Passage birds include sub species B.b.*vulpinus*.

Long-legged Buzzard *Buteo rufinus*
Mainly a scarce winter visitor but now has a toe-hold as a breeding species. Winter sightings usually December to March.

Rough-legged Buzzard *Buteo lagopus*
Accidental . Six winter records, the last in December 1994.

Lesser Spotted Eagle *Aquila pomarina*
Scarce passage migrant. Passes March to May, and September toNovember.

Spotted Eagle *Aquila clanga*
Accidental. Three records only, all in September or October, the last was in 1986.

Imperial Eagle *Aquila heliaca*
Rare breeding resident and probable passage migrant. At least one pair continues to breed in the Troodos Mountains.

Golden Eagle *Aquila chrysaetos*
Accidental. One accepted record from October 1973.

Booted Eagle *Hieraaetus pennatus*
Scarce passage migrant. Passes mainly March to May, and September to October but has occurred in November and December.

Bonelli's Eagle *Hieraaetus fasciatus*
Scarce breeding resident and occasional passage migrant. Small breeding population centred around Paphos Forest. Limited passage March to May, and September to October.

Osprey *Pandion haliaetus*
Passage migrant. Passes in small numbers from April to May; more numerous in autumn from August to October. Has been recorded as early as July and as late as December.

Lesser Kestrel *Falco naumanni*
Passage migrant., rare and occasional winter visitor. Passes in considerably varying numbers, usually more numerous in spring, mainly March to May, and September to early November.

Kestrel *Falco tinnunculus*
Common breeding resident, passage migrant and winter visitor. Passage peaks in April, and again September to October; at other times numbers confused with resident and wintering birds.

Red-footed Falcon *Falco vespertinus*
Common passage migrant. Passes mainly April to May, and September to October; but in some years as early as August and as late as November.

Merlin *Falco columbarius*
Scarce passage migrant and winter visitor between September to April.

Hobby *Falco subbuteo*
Common passage migrant. May have summered and bred in 1995. Passes mainly April to May, and September to October

Eleonora's Falcon *Falco eleonorae*
Breeding migrant in colonies on sea cliffs; has been observed moving on to Turkey in spring. Main influx mid to late April, and main exodus late October.

Sooty Falcon *Falco concolor*
Accidental. One record only in September 1962.

Lanner *Falco biarmicus*
Accidental. Two records only, the last in September 1996.

Saker *Falco cherrug*
Passage migrant. Scarce in spring, passage usually late March to May. Fairly common in autumn between September and October.

Peregrine *Falco peregrinus brookei*
Breeding Resident, passage migrant and winter visitor. Breeds mainly on sea cliffs and inland dams. Passage mainly April to May, and September to October.

Chukar *Alectoris chukar cypriotes*
Common and widespread breeding resident.

Black Francolin *Francolinus francolinus*
Localized but fairly common breeding resident. Population has increased in recent years.

Quail *Coturnix coturnix*
Status uncertain. Present all year, has been known to breed and has been observed migrating from Cape Arnauti. Not certain if there is a resident population.

Water Rail *Rallus aquaticus*
Winter visitor, passage migrant and occasional breeder. Usually present from August to May.

Spotted Crake *Porzana porzana*
Passage migrant. Passes mainly March to May, and September to November; more common in spring.

Little Crake *Porzana parva*
Passage migrant and winter visitor. Passes mainly March to April, and September to November. More common in spring, occasional in winter.

Baillon's Crake *Porzana pusilla intermedia*
Passage migrant and occasional breeder. Scarce and irregular in movements but mainly passes March to May, and September to November.

Corncrake *Crex crex*
Scarce passage migrant. Passes mainly April, and August to November but movements irregular.

Moorhen *Gallinula chloropus*
Passage migrant, winter visitor and increasingly regular breeder.

Allen's Gallinule *Porphyrula alleni*
Accidental. 2 records, in December 1968 and probably relating to the same bird..

Purple Gallinule *Porphyrio porphyrio*
Accidental. Two winter records, the last in 1975.

Coot *Fulica atra*
Passage migrant, winter visitor in varying numbers and increasingly regular breeder.

Common Crane *Grus grus*
Common passage migrant. Passes mainly March to April. and October to November. Spring passage usually in hundreds whereas autumn passage numbered in thousands.

Demoiselle Crane *Anthropoides virgo*
 Passage migrant. Passes March to April, and August to September. Passage heavier in autumn but not in the numbers of Common Crane.

Little Bustard *Tetrax tetrax*
Accidental. One recent winter record only: a single bird near Coral Bay in December 1979.

Houbara Bustard *Chlamydotis undulata macqueenii*
Accidental. Only one recent record: one near Paphos in November 1979 .

Great Bustard *Otis tarda*
Probably now accidental, though in earlier years was an occasional winter visitor. Last record was of 50-60 in early February1974 on the Karpas Peninsula.

Oystercatcher *Haematopus ostralegus*
Scarce passage migrant; mainly in spring from March to May.

Black-winged Stilt *Himantopus himantopus*
Passage migrant and increasingly regular breeding visitor. Passes mainly March to May, and September to November.

Avocet *Recurvirostra avosetta*
Passage migrant and winter visitor in variable numbers. Passes March to May, and August to November.

Stone Curlew *Burhinus oedicnemus saharae*
Localized resident breeding species and common passage migrant. Passes March to May, and September to October.

Cream-coloured Courser *Cursorius cursor*
Scarce and irregular passage migrant, occurring March to May, and in August.

Collared Pratincole *Glareola pratincola*
Fairly common passage migrant. Passes mainly March to May, and August to October.

Collared Pratincole

Oriental Pratincole *Glareola maldivarum*
Accidental. One record only in 1990.

Black-winged Pratincole *Glareola nordmanni*
Passage migrant, usually scarce. Passes mainly April to May, and August to October, normally more numerous in spring.

Little Ringed Plover *Charadrius dubius curonius*
Common passage migrant and limited breeder, occasionally wintering. Passage mainly March to April. and August to October.

Ringed Plover *Charadrius hiaticula*
Passage migrant and winter visitor. Regularly summering and was reported breeding in 1995. Passage mainly March to May, and August to October.

Kittlitz's Plover *Charadrius pecuarius*
Accidental. Four records the last in March 1995.

Kentish Plover *Charadrius alexandrinus*
Breeding resident, breeding migrant, passage migrant and winter visitor. Highest numbers between September to April but no obvious peaks.

Greater Sand Plover *Charadrius leschenaultii colombinus*
Passage migrant and winter visitor. Passage mainly March to April, and August to September. Scarce in winter, has been recorded in every month of the year.

Caspian Plover *Charadrius asiaticus*
Accidental. Seven records mostly in April, the last in April 1996.

Dotterel *Charadrius morinellus*
Scarce and irregular passage migrant in spring and autumn. Occurs mainly March to April, and November to December.

Golden Plover *Pluvialis apricaria*
Winter visitor, possible passage migrant. Occurs mainly October to March, and occasionally August to April.

Grey Plover *Pluvialis squatarola*
Winter visitor and passage migrant in small numbers. Usually occurring from September to May but has been recorded in all months.

Spur-winged Plover *Hoplopterus spinosus*
Passage migrant and localized breeder. Passage mainly March to May, and August to September but now present in all months.

Sociable Plover *Vanellus gregarius*
Accidental. One record only dating from March 1986.

White-tailed Plover *Vanellus leucurus*
Scarce and irregular passage migrant from March to May.

Lapwing *Vanellus vanellus*
Predominately a winter visitor with some passage. Usually recorded from September to April with peak numbers from December to February. Has been recorded earlier and later.

Knot *Calidris canutus*
Scarce and irregular passage migrant. No firm pattern of movement but mainly autumn to winter.

Sanderling *Calidris alba*
Passage migrant and winter visitor. Passes mainly April to May, and September to October. Numbers vary considerably from year to year.

Little Stint *Calidris minuta*
Very common passage migrant, considerably less common in winter. Small numbers of non-breeders summer. Passage mainly April to May, and mid July to October.

Temminck's Stint *Calidris temminckii*
Usually a scarce passage migrant but sometimes in small flocks. Passage mainly April to May, and August to September.

Curlew Sandpiper *Calidris ferruginea*
Passage migrant. Passage mainly April to May, and in lesser numbers from late July to October.

Dunlin *Calidris alpina*
Passage migrant and winter visitor. Occurs August to May in variable numbers.

Broad-billed Sandpiper *Limicola falcinellus*
Scarce passage migrant. Passes mainly April to May, and August to September, often with C. ferruginea and C. alpina.

Ruff *Philomachus pugnax*
Very common passage migrant and considerably less common winter visitor. Main passage occurs March to May and in September, but has been recorded in all months of the year.

Jack Snipe *Lymnocryptes minimus*
Passage migrant and winter visitor in small numbers. Winter visitors usually present from November to February and on passage March to April, and October.

Common Snipe *Gallinago gallinago*
Passage migrant and winter visitor in variable numbers. Usually present from August to May, has been recorded in all months of the year. Passage most pronounced from March to April.

Great Snipe *Gallinago media*
Passage migrant. In recent years spring movement only from March to May.

Woodcock *Scolopax rusticola*
Winter visitor in variable numbers, usually occurring between November and February.

Black-tailed Godwit *Limosa limosa*
Passage migrant and winter visitor. Has been recorded in all months but most numerous on passage from February to May and to a lesser degree in September.

Bar-tailed Godwit *Limosa lapponica*
Scarce and irregular passage migrant.

Whimbel *Numenius phaeopus*
Scarce and irregular passage migrant, usuually occurring from April to May, and August to October.

Slender-billed Curlew *Numenius tenuirostris*
Accidental. Three records only, the last in April 1972.

Curlew *Numenius arquata*
Passage migrant and winter visitor. Occurs mainly from September to May but occasionally from late July. Most sightings post December.

Spotted Redshank *Tringa erythropus*
Passage migrant and scarce winter visitor. Passes mainly March to May, and September to October. Singletons randomly recorded in winter.

Common Redshank *Tringa totanus*
Winter visitor and passage migrant in variable numbers with a small number of non-breeders summering. Usually arrives from late June: winter visitors peak from December to January and most depart in March with passage migrants.

Marsh Sandpiper *Tringa stagnatilis*
Passage migrant. Common on spring migration from mid March to late May, peaking in April. Scarce on autumn passage, mainly July to September.

Greenshank *Tringa nebularia*
Passage migrant and winter visitor. Passes mainly March to May, and July to September. Winter movements erratic; sometimes summers.

Green Sandpiper *Tringa ochropus*
Passage migrant and winter visitor. Passes mainly March to April, and July to September in considerable numbers; scarcer in winter. In many years recorded in every month.

Wood Sandpiper *Tringa glareola*
Common passage migrant, occasional winter visitor. Passes mainly March to May, and July to October. Increasingly recorded in most months of the year.

Terek Sandpiper *Xenus cinereus*
Occasional passage migrant. More sightings in recent years has elevated the status from 'Accidental'; it continues to be rare though perhaps overlooked. Last record in 1993.

Common Sandpiper *Actitis hypoleucos*
Common passage migrant and winter visitor in limited numbers. Passes mainly March to May, and July to September. Now regularly recorded in every month of the year.

Turnstone *Arenaria interpres*
Scarce passage migrant, occasionally wintering. Passes mainly April to May, and August to October. Has been recorded in every month of the year.

Red-necked Phalarope *Phalaropus lobatus*
Scarce passage migrant. Passes mainly April to May, and August to September.

Arctic Skua *Stercorarius parasiticus*
Scarce and irregular passage migrant, perhaps overlooked. Mostly recorded March to May and less often September to November.

Great Black-headed Gull *Larus ichthyaetus*
Occasional. To date there are 10+ records, mainly in winter and early spring

Mediterranean Gull *Larus melanocephalus*
Winter visitor and passage migrant. Occurs mainly between November and May.

Little Gull *Larus minutus*
Winter visitor and passage migrant. Occurs mainly December to April but occasionally earlier and later: sometimes in hundreds.

Black-headed Gull *Larus ridibundus*
Predominately a winter visitor; some passage. Mainly November to March peaking in December. Small parties recorded in all other months.

Slender-billed Gull *Larus genei*
Common passage migrant and scarce winter visitor. Passes mainly April to May, and July to October, sometimes in hundreds to thousands. Scarce in winter; has been recorded in every month of the year.

Audouin's Gull *Larus audouinii*
Status uncertain but is either a resident or migrant breeder. Breeds on a few small offshore islets. Seen in all months except November.

Common Gull *Larus canus*
Scarce winter visitor occurring mainly November to April.

Lesser Black-backed Gull *Larus fuscus*
Passage migrant and winter visitor. Passes mainly March to May, and August to October; usually scarce in other months.

Herring Gull *Larus argentatus*
Accidental. One record only dating from 1990.

Yellow-legged Gull *Larus cachinnans*
Resident breeder, winter visitor and possible passage migrant. Breeds on cliffs and offshore islands. Post breeding flocks form from June onwards and are swelled by winter visitors from November to April.

Armenian Gull *Larus armenicus*
Winter visitor and passage migrant. Small numbers recorded randomly from December to May.

Great Black-backed Gull *Larus marinus*
Accidental. Six records only, the last in February 1996.

Kittiwake *Rissa tridactyla*
Accidental. Two records only, both in 1961.

Gull-billed Tern *Sterna nilotica*
Passage migrant. Passes mainly March to May, and August to September in far fewer numbers.

Caspian Tern *Sterna caspia*
Scarce passage migrant. Passes April to May, and August to September.

Sandwich Tern *Sterna sandvicensis*
Winter visitor and passage migrant. Occurs between December and April in variable numbers.

Common Tern *Sterna hirundo*
Common passage migrant and occasional in winter. Passes April to May in substantial numbers, and from August to October although scarce and irregular in autumn.

Arctic Tern *Sterna paradisaea*
Accidental. Three records only, all in spring, the last in 1984.

Little Tern *Sterna albifrons*
Scarce passage migrant. Passes mainly March to May, and irregularly August to September.

Whiskered Tern *Chlidonias hybridus*
Passage migrant in small numbers. Passes early March to May, and July to October.

Black Tern *Chlidonias niger*
Passage migrant. Passes mainly March to May, and July to October, occasionally to November.

White-winged Black Tern *Chlidonias leucopterus*
Common passage migrant. Passes mainly April to May, and July to August; earlier and later records not uncommon.

Black-bellied Sandgrouse *Pterocles orientalis*
Scarce resident breeder confined to south-west Mesaoria (the central plain).

Pin-tailed Sandgrouse *Pterocles alchata caudacutus*
No records this century, the last in 1820.

Rock Dove *Columba livia gaddi*
Common breeding resident on offshore islands, sea cliffs and inland ravines.

Stock Dove *Columba oenas*
Winter visitor and possible passage migrant. Variable in numbers most occurring November to April.

Woodpigeon *Columba palumbus*
Breeding resident. Present in small numbers in inland wooded areas, sometimes flocking in substantial numbers in winter.

Collared Dove *Streptopelia decaocta*
Breeding resident. Has become increasingly common and widespread in recent years.

Turtle Dove *Streptopelia turtur*
Very common passage migrant with many staying to breed. Arrives mainly April and departs September with stragglers to November.

Laughing Dove *Streptopelia senegalensis*
Accidental. Last confirmed record 1968 but other more recent, unsubstantiated sightings.

Great-spotted Cuckoo *Clamator glandarius*
Passage migrant with some staying to breed. Passes mainly March to May, departing August. There is no autumn passage: parasitic on Magpies.

Didric Cuckoo *Chrysococcyx caprius*
Accidental. One at Akrotiri on 27th June 1982 was the first record for the Palearctic.

Cuckoo *Cuculus canorus*
Passage migrant, possibly occasionally remaining to breed. Common in spring, passing mainly March to May. Scarce and irregular in autumn but recorded between July and November.

Barn Owl *Tyto alba*
Widespread breeding resident.

Scops Owl *Otus scops*
Widespread breeding resident and passage migrant. Passes mainly March to April, and September to October (data based on limestick casualties and ringing records).

Little Owl *Athene noctua*
Widespread breeding resident. up to mid-levels.

Long-eared Owl *Asio otus*
Status uncertain. Is known to be a breeding resident but may also be a winter visitor and passage migrant. Has been recorded throughout the island.

Short-eared Owl *Asio flammeus*
Scarce passage migrant and winter visitor occurring from September to April.

Nightjar *Caprimulgus europaeus*
Common passage migrant and migrant breeder. Passes mainly April to May, and August to early November.

Common Swift *Apus apus*
Very common passage migrant and migrant breeder. Occurs as early as late January but main spring passage is March to April. Return movement is from June to September with stragglers in October and occasionally later.

Pallid Swift *Apus pallidus*
Migrant breeder; occasional limited passage. Arrives March to April, and departs progressively from August to October.

Alpine Swift *Apus melba*
Migrant breeder and passage migrant. Main arrival February to March, departing August to September. Large numbers pass on spring passage from February to May, but autumn passage is weak and ill-defined and masked by departing breeders.

Little Swift *Apus affinis*
Occasional but records increasing year by year in the spring, possibly due to greater observer coverage of the south coast.

White-breasted Kingfisher *Halcyon smyrnensis*
A number of sightings in recent years has raised the status from Accidental to Occasional winter visitor. last record 1993.

Common Kingfisher *Alcedo atthis*
Passage migrant and winter visitor. Most common on passage August to October, and March to April but recorded in all months except June.

Pied Kingfisher *Ceryle rudis*
Mainly winter visitor but has been recorded in every month of the year and has attempted to breed (1996). Sightings have increased in recent years.

Blue-cheeked Bee-eater *Merops persicus*
Scarce passage migrant. Passes March to May, and less frequently September to October.

European Bee-eater *Merops apiaster*
Very common passage migrant and scarce migrant breeder. Passes mainly April to May , sometimes in continuous streams of thousands; and from late July to October in lesser numbers.

Roller *Coracias garrulus*
Passage migrant and migrant breeder. Passes mainly late March to May, and August to October. Has wintered.

Hoopoe *Upupa epops*
Passage migrant and migrant breeder. Passes mainly late March to early May, and August to October. Has been recorded as late as November, and as early as January.

Wryneck *Jynx torquilla*
Passage migrant and scarce winter visitor. Passes March to May, and August to October. Winter records in January and February.

Desert Lark *Ammomanes deserti*
Accidental. One record dating from April 1973.

Dupont's Lark *Chersophilus duponti*
Accidental. One record dating from April 1994.

Calandra Lark *Melanocorypha calandra*
Common resident, passage migrant and possible winter visitor. Localized breeder on flat arable land. Post-breeding dispersal in large flocks. Passes late February to April; no noticable autumn passage.

Bimaculated Lark *Melanocorypha bimaculata*
Passage migrant, passing in small numbers April to May. Perhaps overlooked or confused with Calandra Lark.

Short-toed Lark *Calandrella brachydactyla*
Common migrant breeder and passage migrant. Present from March to November but has been recorded in January. Passes March to May in large numbers sometimes in hundreds, and August to November usually in tens.

Lesser Short-toed Lark *Calandrella rufescens*
Passage migrant and possible winter visitor. Scarce and irregular from November to April with most sightings occurring between February and April.

Crested Lark *Galerida cristata cypriaca*
Very common and widespread resident breeder, and passage migrant from March to April. Post breeding dispersal occurs in some lowland areas from June to September.

Woodlark *Lullula arborea pallida*
Resident breeder, winter visitor and possible passage migrant. Some clinal variations but breeds mainly above 600m. Descends in winter.

Skylark *Alauda arvensis cantarella*
Common winter visitor and autumn passage migrant but bred in 1997 at Kiti dam. Mainly arriving October and departing February, but most years stragglers remain until April.

Shore Lark *Eremophila alpestris*
Accidental. Two records only, the last dating from 1992.

Sand Martin *Riparia riparia*
Very common passage migrant. Passes mainly March to May, and August to October; earlier and later dates not uncommon. Has occurred in every month of the year.

Crag Martin *Ptyonoprogne rupestris*
Resident breeder and limited passage migrant. localized breeding mainly in the mountains descending to the lowlands in winter. Passage February to April and probably in October.

Swallow *Hirundo rustica*
Common migrant breeder and passage migrant. Passes February to May in very large numbers, and August to October. Post breeding roosts in reedbeds are swollen by passage migrants and contain many thousands.

Red-rumped Swallow *Hirundo daurica*
Common migrant breeder and passage migrant. Passes mainly March to April, and August to September, but sightings in all months of the year.

House Martin *Delichon urbica*
Common but localized migrant breeder, and common spring migrant. First arrivals usually in February with main passage April to May. Breeding birds depart mainly July to August; occasionally passage noted to October.

Richard's Pipit *Anthus novaeseelandiae richardi*
Scarce and irregular passage migrant. Mainly recorded March to May, and randomly from October to December.

Tawny Pipit *Anthus campestris*
Passage migrant, occasionally seen in winter. Passes mainly March to May, and in fewer numbers from September to November. Has been recorded in December and January.

Long-billed Pipit *Anthus similis captus*
Accidental. One record only dating from April 1972.

Olive-backed Pipit *Anthus hodgsoni yunnanensis*
Accidental. One record only dating from February 1989.

Tree Pipit *Anthus trivialis*
Passage migrant. Common in spring passing mainly March to April, less into May. Autumn passage from September to October, occasionally November but in much reduced numbers.

Meadow Pipit *Anthus pratensis*
Winter visitor and limited passage migrant. Occasionally September but mainly October to April with fewer in May. Passage observed February to March, and late October to November.

Red-throated Pipit *Anthus cervinus*
Passage migrant and winter visitor. Passes March to May in hundreds, and September to October when again numerous. Winter numbers variable but usually small.

Water Pipit *Anthus spinoletta*
Passage migrant and winter visitor. Common on passage March to April, less so on autumn passage October to November. Winter numbers variable but never common.

Yellow Wagtail *Motacilla flava*
Passage Migrant and migrant breeder. 7 races recorded on passage but only 3 regularly: Blue-headed, Grey-headed and Black-headed. Passage mainly March to May, and August to October.

Black-headed Wagtail *Motacilla flava feldegg*
Localized breeding migrant and passage migrant. Present March to October.

Citrine Wagtail *Motacilla citreola*
Passage migrant , increasingly reported. Sightings mainly March to May, and September.

Grey Wagtail *Motacilla cinerea*
Winter visitor, passage migrant and possible occasional breeder. Arrives August and usually departs in April. Passage seems limited to autumn, mainly October to early December. Juveniles observed in summer but no positive proof of breeding.

White Wagtail *Motacilla alba*
Common winter visitor and passage migrant, has bred. Present August to May: spring passage March to May, and autumn September to November.

Waxwing *Bombycilla garrulus*
Accidental. One record of five birds dating from January1966; an invasion year across Europe.

Dipper *Cinclus cinclus*
No sightings since 1945. Formerly bred in Paphos Forest.

Wren *Troglodytes troglodytes cypriotes*
Resident breeder in the highlands where often common in valley bottoms near streams. Some dispersal to lowlands in winter may mask winter visitors.

Dunnock *Prunella modularis*
Winter visitor and possible passage migrant. Present in variable numbers from October to April. Maybe some passage in November.

Rufous Bush Robin *Cercotrichas galactotes syriacus*
Scarce passage migrant.Passes March to May, and August to October.

Robin *Erithacus rubecula*
Winter visitor, very common and widespread; some evidence of passage. Mainly arrives October departs April. Passage in November and March.

Thrush Nightingale *Luscinia luscinia*
Common passage migrant. Passage from March to April, and August to October. Status assessed mainly by liming and ringing studies. Sight records relatively few suggesting probable confusion with Nightingale.

Nightingale *Luscinia megarhynchos*
Common migrant breeder and passage migrant. Breeds mainly above 800m. Numerous on spring passage from March to May, scarce on passage in autumn from August to October.

Bluethroat *Luscinia svecica*
Passage migrant and winter visitor. Present from September to April. Passage mainly October to November, no significant spring passage. Winters mainly in reedbeds.

Red-flanked Bluetail *Tarsiger cyanurus*
Accidental. Two records , the last in October 1987.

White-throated Robin *Irania gutturalis*
Occasional. There are six records only, during March to April.

Black Redstart *Phoenicurus ochuros gibraltariensis*
Common winter visitor and passage migrant. Mainly present from October to April but early arrivals sometimes appear in September and stragglers remain into May. Passage mainly March and October.

Common Redstart *Phoenicurus phoenicurus*
Passage migrant. Passes mainly March to May, and August to October with stragglers to November. Has been recorded in January and February.

Whinchat *Saxicola rubetra*
Passage migrant. Passes mainly March to May, and August to November with stragglers into December.

Stonechat *Saxicola torquata rubicola*
Common and widespread winter visitor. Arrives late September and departs progressively from February to April.

Pied Stonechat *Saxicola caprata*
Accidental. One record dating from November 1986.

Isabelline Wheatear *Oenanthe isabellina*
Common passage migrant. Passes mainly late February to April, sometimes May, and August to November; less common in autumn.

Isabelline Wheatear

Northern Wheatear *Oenanthe oenanthe*
Passage migrant, common in spring. Passes mainly February to May; less common in autumn passing August to November. Has been recorded as early as January and as late as December.

Pied Wheatear *Oenanthe pleschanka*
Accidental. One record dating from 1992

Cyprus Pied Wheatear *Oenanthe cypriaca*
Migrant breeder. Abundant and widespread, mainly present March to October but sometimes into November, and has occurred in January and February.

Black-eared Wheatear *Oenanthe hispanica*
Passage migrant. Passes mainly March to May and is fairly common; very scarce in autumn passing August to November.

Desert Wheatear *Oenanthe deserti*
Scarce passage migrant, in spring from March to April; scarcer in autumn from August to October. Usually of single birds only.

Finsch's Wheatear *Oenanthe finschii*
Winter visitor and passage migrant. Arrives late September to early October, and departs progressively February to March. Occasional singles April to May suggest a limited passage occurs.

Red-tailed Wheatear *Oenanthe xanthoprymna*
Accidental. One record only dating from 1991

Mourning Wheatear *Oenanthe lugens*
Accidental. One record only dating from 1991.

Hooded Wheatear *Oenanthe monacha*
Accidental. Six recent records only, the latest in April and May 1996.

White-crowned Wheatear *Oenanthe leucopyga*
Accidental. Three records only, the last in 1993.

Rock Thrush *Monticola saxatilis*
Scare passage migrant. Passes mainly March to April but occasionally February to May. Infrequently in autumn from September to November. Has been recorded in June and July.

Blue Rock Thrush *Monticola solitarius*
Localized common breeding resident, winter visitor and passage migrant. Winter visitors arrive September to October and remain until early April. Passage (detected by liming activity) occurs from February to April.

Ring Ouzel *Turdus torquatus*
Scarce and irregular passage migrant and winter visitor. Recorded September to March and most frequently in November, usually in the mountains.

Blackbird *Turdus merula*
Winter visitor, passage migrant and possible scarce resident breeder. Arrives October to November, and departs progressively from February to April. Surges in numbers during February to March probably indicate passage; no noticeable autumn passage. Presence in mountains in summer suggests possible breeding.

Dusky Thrush *Turdus naumanni*
Accidental. Three records only, the last dating from November 1993.

Fieldfare *Turdus pilaris*
Winter visitor in variable numbers. Mainly October to February with singles lingering into April, sometimes May.

Song Thrush *Turdus philomelos*
Very common winter visitor and probable passage migrant. Mainly October to April but sometimes earlier and lingering into May. Roosts sometimes number thousands. Liming studies suggest some passage during March.

Redwing *Turdus iliacus*
Winter visitor and passage migrant in variable numbers but usually scarce. Occurs mainly November to March with passage November to January.

Mistle Thrush *Turdus viscivorus*
Winter visitor and passage migrant in variable numbers. Occurs mainly October to March; passage mainly November.

Cetti's Warbler *Cettia cetti*
Common and widespread breeding resident, mainly below 600m; some dispersal in winter.

Fan-tailed Warbler *Cisticola juncidis*
Common and widespread breeding resident . Especially favouring areas up to 500 m where cereals, tall grass and other dense vegetation may be found.

Graceful Warbler *Prinia gracilis*
Accidental. One record only dating from October 1987.

Grasshopper Warbler *Locustella naevia*
Accidental. One record only dating from September 1968.

River Warbler *Locustella fluviatilis*
Scarce passage migrant. Seldom seen, skulking behaviour probably causes it to be overlooked but ringing records suggests passage April, and August to October.

Savi's Warbler *Locustella luscinioides*
Passage migrant. Passes March to April, and late July to November.

Moustached Warbler *Acrocephalus melanopogon*
Winter visitor to reedbeds. Arrives October and departs mainly March to April.

Sedge Warbler *Acrocephalus schoenobaenus*
Passage migrant in variable numbers. Passes mainly March to May, and July to November.

Marsh Warbler *Acrocephalus palustris*
Passage migrant. Spring passage extremely sparse, mainly April but has been recorded in May. Fairly common in autumn, passes mainly September to October.

Reed Warbler *Acrocephalus scirpaceus fuscus*
Locally common migrant breeder and passage migrant. Arrives mainly March and departs progressively from August to November with sightings in some years extending to December. Passes March to May, and August to November.

Great Reed Warbler *Acrocephalus arundinaceus*
Fairly common passage migrant and occasional breeder. Passes late March to early May but mainly April, and August to October.

Basra Reed Warbler *Acrocephalus griseldis*
Vagrant. One record dating from 1981

Olivaceous Warbler *Hippolais pallida*
Common and widespread migrant breeder and passage migrant. Present in most years from March to October, occasionally November. Main influx and passage in April; autumn passage from August to October.

Olive-tree Warbler *Hippolais olivetorum*
Very scarce passage migrant, perhaps overlooked. Passes April to May, and August to September.

Icterine Warbler *Hippolais icterina*
Scarce passage migrant. Passes April to May, and August to October.

Spectacled Warbler *Sylvia conspicillata*
Resident breeder favouring arid ground up to 500 m.

Subalpine Warbler *Sylvia cantillans*
Spring passage migrant in variable numbers. Passes March to April.

Sardinian Warbler *Sylvia melanocephala*
Winter visitor and localized breeding resident. Winter visitors arrive mainly October and

depart progressively March to April. First recorded as breeding on the Akamas peninsular in 1992, now breeds in numbers and is rapidly expanding its range southwards.

Cyprus Warbler *Sylvia melanothorax*
Resident and migrant breeder. Largely absent from the Mesaoria region but otherwise widespread up to 1,400 m. Departs mainly September to October, and returns February to March after wintering in Lebanon and Palestine.

Rüppell's Warbler *Sylvia rueppelli*
Passage migrant. Passes mainly March to April with stragglers into May. Fairly common in spring but extremely scarce in autumn sometimes occurring between August and November.

Desert Warbler *Sylvia nana*
Accidental. Five records, the last in March 1995.

Orphean Warbler *Sylvia hortensis crassirostris*
Passage migrant. Common in spring passing mainly March to April and occasionally May. Scarce in autumn passing August to October.

Barred Warbler *Sylvia nisoria*
Passage migrant. Liming kills in 1968 and recent studies in spring on the Akamas peninsular suggest that it is less scarce than previously thought. Passes March to May, and August to October.

Lesser Whitethroat *Sylvia curruca*
Very common passage migrant. Passes mainly March to May, and August to October, but sightings both earlier and later are not infrequent.

Common Whitethroat *Sylvia communis*
Common passage migrant. Passes mainly March to May , fewer numbers August to October. Earlier and later sightings not uncommon.

Garden Warbler *Sylvia borin*
Passage migrant in variable numbers, usually fairly common. Passes mainly April to May, and August to October.

Blackcap *Sylvia atricapilla*
Very common passage migrant, winter visitor and may occasionally breed. Passes March to May, and August to November. Fairly common winter visitor from November to March below 800 m.

Yellow-browed Warbler *Phylloscopus inornatus*
Accidental. Late autumn vagrant. six records the last in 1993.

Dusky Warbler *Phylloscopus fuscatus*
Accidental. One record dating from September 1967.

Bonelli's Warbler *Phylloscopus bonelli orientalis*
Passage migrant in markedly variable numbers, especially in spring. Passes March to May but mainly April, and September to October when it is scarce and irregular.

Wood Warbler *Phylloscopus sibilatrix*
Passage migrant in variable numbers. Passes mainly March to May, and in considerably lesser numbers from August to October.

Chiffchaff *Phylloscopus collybita*
Very common passage migrant and winter visitor. Present mainly September to April with passage peaks in November and March.

Willow Warbler *Phylloscopus trochilus*
Passage migrant. Passes mainly March to May, and August to November; has been recorded in all months of the year.

Goldcrest *Regulus regulus*
Winter visitor. Mainly November to March, sometimes April, favouring pine forest at all levels.

Firecrest *Regulus ignicapillus*
Accidental. Two records, both from the Troodos mountains, the last dating from February 1962.

Spotted Flycatcher *Muscicapa striata neumanni*
Localized migrant breeder and passage migrant. Present March to October breeding mainly in pine forest above 900 m. Passes March to May, and August to October.

Red-breasted Flycatcher *Ficedula parva*
Very scarce and irregular passage migrant. Few sightings in spring (April) but fairly regular in autumn between September to November.

Semi-collared Flycatcher *Ficedula semitorquata*
Assessed as a scarce passage migrant in spring passing March to May, but likely confusion with Pied Flycatcher in some plumages may lead to it being overlooked.

Collared Flycatcher *Ficedula albicollis*
Passage migrant in spring in variable numbers. Passes March to May.

Pied Flycatcher *Ficedula hypoleuca*
Passage migrant in spring in variable numbers, rarely and randomly in autumn. Passes mainly March to May; a few records only in September and October.

Bearded Tit *Panurus biarmicus*
Irregular winter visitor, mainly to reedbeds, occurring October to March.

Coal Tit *Parus ater cypriotes*
Common breeding resident in the foothills and mountains.

Great Tit *Parus major*
Common and fairly widespread breeding resident.

Wallcreeper *Tichodroma muraria*
Winter visitor. Occurs mainly October to March, sometimes April; frequenting cliffs, rock faces and stone buildings.

Short-toed Treecreeper *Certhia brachydactyla dorotheae*
Common breeding resident in pine forests of foothills and mountains.

Penduline Tit *Remiz pendulinus*
Winter visitor and almost certainly occasional breeder. Present mainly October to March, has been seen in July and with fledged juveniles in August.

Golden Oriole *Oriolus oriolus*
Passage migrant and scarce irregular breeder. Present March to October, passes mainly April to May, often in substantial numbers. Less common in autumn from August to October, mainly September.

Isabelline Shrike *Lanius isabellinus*
Accidental. Five records only, the last in May 1996.

Red-backed Shrike *Lanius collurio*
Passage migrant in variable numbers but usually common. Passes mainly April to May, and August to November but has been recorded in all months of the year and may be an occasional breeder, though no positive evidence to date.

Lesser Grey Shrike *Lanius minor*
Passage migrant in variable numbers. Passes mainly late March to May, and August to late September with stragglers into October and November.

Lesser Grey Shrike

Great Grey Shrike *Lanius excubitor*
Accidental. One record only, dating from April 1989.

Woodchat Shrike *Lanius senator*
Passage migrant, occasional breeder. Present March to October with main passage April to May, but scarce and irregular from August to October.

Masked Shrike *Lanius nubicus*
Common migrant breeder in foothills and mountains, and passage migrant. Present March to October. Passes mainly April but no obvious passage peaks; movements blurred by migrant breeders.

Jay *Garrulus glandarius glaszneri*
Common resident in Troodos mountains, less common in Paphos Forest down to 500 m. Evidence suggests occasional vagrancy perhaps from Turkey.

Magpie *Pica pica*
Common resident and probable winter visitor. Favours lightly wooded areas and therefore scarce in the Mesaoria region but common elsewhere. Migratory movements observed from Cape Andreas towards Turkey.

Jackdaw *Corvus monedula soemmerringii*
Common localized resident and probable winter visitor. Favours cliffs and rocky valleys for breeding. Some post-breeding dispersal and flocking. Evidence suggests some winter visitors from the north of Europe.

Rook *Corvus frugilegus*
Irregular winter visitor occurring mainly January to May.

Hooded Crow *Corvus corone sardonius*
Common and widespread resident away from pine forests and below 1,000 m.

Raven *Corvus corax*
Once a common resident now considerably less so. Mainly on sea cliffs, rocky ravines or mountains.

Starling *Sturnus vulgaris*
Very common winter visitor and passage migrant, Usually first appears in October with main influx November; main departure February but stragglers sometimes stay till May. Some passage in November and March.

Rose-coloured Starling *Sturnus roseus*
Very scarce and irregular passage migrant occurring April, May and August. Last sighting 30th April to 5th May 1997.

House Sparrow *Passer domesticus biblicus*
Very common resident, passage migrant and probable winter visitor. From liming catches and observation there is evidence of passage and likelihood of resident population supplemented by winter visitors.

Spanish Sparrow *Passer hispaniolensis*
Locally fairly common resident, very common passage migrant and fairly common winter visitor. Passes mainly September to October, and March to May sometimes in thousands.

Dead Sea Sparrow *Passer moabiticus*
Status uncertain. First recorded in 1980 and bred the same year. By 1982 a colony of at least 16 pairs was established in the Akrotiri reedbeds, but in subsequent years the colony declined and there has been no evidence of recent breeding; however sightings continue randomly.

Tree Sparrow *Passer montanus*
Scarce winter visitor occurring between October and April.

Pale Rock Sparrow *Petronia brachydactyla*
Accidental. Three spring records since 1991, the last in March 1995.

Rock Sparrow *Petronia petronia*
Accidental. Three records, the last in April 1997.

Chaffinch *Fringilla coelebs*
Common resident, passage migrant and winter visitor. Breeds mainly in pine forests and orchards in the Troodos mountains and foothills. Numerous on passage February to April, and October to November, Common winter visitor October to February.

Brambling *Fringilla montifringilla*
Scarce winter visitor from October to March.

Red-fronted Serin *Serinus pusillus*
Accidental. Four records, the last two were in March and December 1994.

Serin *Serinus serinus*
Resident, winter visitor and passage migrant. Breeding is localized; winter visitors are widespread and often numerous. Arrives October and departs mainly March to April. Passage is concurrent.

Greenfinch *Carduelis chloris*
Resident, winter visitor and passage migrant. Breeding is general and widespread. Winter visitors arrive October to November, and depart February to March. Passes February to April, and October to November.

Goldfinch *Carduelis carduelis niediecki*
Very common and widespread resident, winter visitor and passage migrant. Common winter visitor with peak numbers November to February. Passes mainly February to April, and October to November.

Siskin *Carduelis spinus*
Winter visitor in variable numbers. Occurs mainly October to April.

Linnet *Carduelis cannabina*
Resident, winter visitor and passage migrant. Breeds widely and generally. Common winter visitor from November to March. Passes February to April, and October to November.

Common Redpoll *Carduelis flammea*
Accidental. Six winter records, the last in 1992.

Common Crossbill *Loxia curvirostra guillemardi*
Localized resident and possible winter visitor. Breeds in the Troodos range, there is some post-breeding dispersal to lower levels otherwise sedentary.

Trumpeter Finch *Bucanetes githagineus*
Occasional in spring from March to April.

Scarlet Rosefinch *Carpodacus erythrinus*
Accidental. Four records only, the last in December 1982.

Hawfinch *Coccothraustes coccothraustes*
Scarce winter visitor occurring from October to April.

Pine Bunting *Emberiza leucocephalos*
Accidental. Four records only, the last was at Cape Andreas (the eastern extremity of the Turkish Cypriot controlled area of the island) in March 1996. The last sighting in the Greek Cypriot sector was of 14 near Stavrovouni in January 1976 dwindling to one in February 1976.

Yellowhammer *Emberiza citrinella*
Occasional scarce winter visitor. last recorded in March 1996.

Rock Bunting *Emberiza cia*
Very scarce and irregular spring migrant, occurring March to April. Once in January.

Cinereous Bunting *Emberiza cineracea*
Scarce passage migrant in spring (possibly overlooked in concurrent large movements of Ortolan Bunting). Passes March to April.

Ortolan Bunting *Emberiza hortulana*
Common passage migrant. Passes March to May, and mainly August to September.

Cretzschmar's Bunting *Emberiza caesia*
Widespread migrant breeder and passage migrant. Passes March to April. Autumn movements masked by migrant breeder exodus from August to September.

Yellow-breasted Bunting *Emberiza aureola*
Accidental. One record dating from May 1974.

Reed Bunting *Emberiza schoeniclus*
Common winter visitor, occasionally from September but mainly October, departing February to March.

Black-headed Bunting

Black-headed Bunting *Emberiza melanocephala*
Migrant breeder and passage migrant. Localized common to very common breeder. Arrives April and departs unobtrusively from July. Passes April to May; no autumn passage detected.

Corn Bunting *Miliaria calandra*
Resident, passage migrant and winter visitor. Widespread breeding favouring cereals and vineyards. Common on passage between February and May, and October to November. Winter visitor arrival and departure coincides with autumn and spring passage.

Checklist of the Birds of Cyprus

This list follows the order of Voous and the chosen English names are those preferred by the authors.

The list includes only species accepted by Flint and Stewart in The birds of Cyprus, B.O.U Check-list No 6. and subsequent additions agreed by the Cyprus Ornithological Society (1957) Rarities Committee.

The abbreviated status codes used below generally follow The Birds of Cyprus B.O.U. Check-list (Flint & Stewart) but they are greatly simplified and The Systematic Synopsis of Cyprus Records expands on the status of the species listed here.

The status of species is periodically reviewed by the Rarities Committee as the influences of man and nature separately and collectively affect bird populations and as knowledge of the island's ornithology grows.

Any species not listed here but which are observed by visitors to the island are likely to be vagrants or escaped birds and records should be accompanied with full details and descriptions obtained in the field.

Records of all sightings, especially those of rarities are welcomed by the Cyprus Ornithological Society (1957) and should be sent to the Recorder at Yiangou Souroulla 6, 6037 Larnaca, Cyprus.

Note: Species marked * require field notes for all sightings and those marked ** require descriptions when seen in autumn.

RB Resident Breeder   WV Winter Visitor

MB Migrant Breeder   OV Occasional Visitor (more than 6 but less than 12 records)

OB Occasional Breeder   AV Accidental Visitor (up to 6 records)

PM Passage Migrant   SU Status Uncertain

				English name	Scientific name	Status
				Diver sp.*	*Gavia sp*	AV
✓				Little Grebe	*Tachybaptus ruficollis*	WV,PM,OB
✓	✓			Great Crested Grebe	*Podiceps cristatus*	WV,PM,OB
				Red-necked Grebe*	*Podiceps grisegena*	AV
				Slavonian Grebe*	*Podiceps auritus*	AV
✓				Black-necked Grebe	*Podiceps nigricollis*	WV,OB
				Cory's Shearwater	*Calonectris diomedea*	PM
				Mediterranean Shearwater	*Puffinus yelkouan*	PM
				Storm Petrel*	*Hydrobates pelagicus*	AV
				Gannet	*Morus bassanus*	PM (irregular)
✓	✓			Cormorant	*Phalacrocorax carbo*	WV,PM
✓	✓			Shag	*Phalacrocorax aristotelis*	RB
				Pygmy Cormorant*	*Phalacrocorax pygmeus*	WV
				White Pelican	*Pelecanus onocratalus*	PM
				Dalmatian Pelican*	*Pelecanus crispus*	PM
				Bittern	*Botaurus stellaris*	PM,WV
				Little Bittern	*Ixobrychus minutus*	PM,OB?
				Night Heron	*Nycticorax nycticorax*	PM,OB
				Squacco Heron	*Ardeola ralloides*	PM
✓	✓			Cattle Egret	*Bubulcus ibis*	PM

						English name	Scientific name	Status
						Little Egret	*Egretta garzetta*	PM,WV,OB
						Great White Egret	*Egretta alba*	PM,WV
✓	✓					Grey Heron	*Ardea cinerea*	PM,WV
						Purple Heron	*Ardea purpurea*	PM
						Black Stork	*Ciconia nigra*	PM
						White Stork	*Ciconia ciconia*	PM
						Glossy Ibis	*Plegadis falcinellus*	PM
						Spoonbill	*Platalea leucorodia*	PM
✓	✓					Greater Flamingo	*Phoenicopterus ruber*	WV,PM
						Mute Swan	*Cygnus olor*	WV
						Whooper Swan*	*Cygnus cygnus*	AV
						White-fronted Goose	*Anser albifrons*	WV
✓						Greylag Goose*	*Anser anser*	WV
						Red-breasted Goose*	*Branta ruficollis*	AV
						Egyptian Goose*	*Alopochen aegyptiacus*	AV
						Ruddy Shelduck	*Tadorna ferruginea*	WV
						Shelduck	*Tadorna tadorna*	WV,PM
✓	✓					Wigeon	*Anas penelope*	WV,PM
						Gadwall	*Anas strepera*	WV,PM
✓	✓					Teal	*Anas crecca*	WV,PM
✓	✓					Mallard	*Anas platyrhynchos*	WV,PM,OB
	✓					Pintail	*Anas acuta*	WV,PM
						Garganey	*Anas querquedula*	PM,OB
	✓					Shoveler	*Anas clypeata*	WV,PM
						Marbled Duck*	*Marmaronetta angustirostris*	OV
	✓					Red-crested Pochard	*Netta rufina*	WV
✓	✓					Pochard	*Aythya ferina*	WV,PM
						Ferruginous Duck	*Aythya nyroca*	WV,PM,OB?
	✓					Tufted Duck	*Aythya fuligula*	WV,PM
						Scaup*	*Aythya marila*	AV
						Common Scoter*	*Melanitta nigra*	AV
						Goldeneye*	*Bucephala clangula*	AV
						Smew*	*Mergellus albellus*	AV
						Red-breasted Merganser	*Mergus serrator*	WV
						Goosander*	*Mergus merganser*	AV
						White-headed Duck*	*Oxyura leucocephala*	WV,PM?
						Honey Buzzard	*Pernis apivorus*	PM
	✓					Black Kite	*Milvus migrans*	PM
						Red Kite*	*Milvus milvus*	AV
						White-tailed Eagle*	*Haliaeetus albicilla*	AV
						Lammergeier*	*Gypaetus barbatus*	AV
						Egyptian Vulture*	*Neophron percnopterus*	PM
✓						Griffon Vulture	*Gyps fulvus*	RB,PM
						Black Vulture*	*Aegypius monachus*	SU
						Short-toed Eagle*	*Circaetus gallicus*	PM
	✓					Marsh Harrier	*Circus aeruginosus*	PM,WV
✓	✓					Hen Harrier	*Circus cyaneus*	WV,PM
						Pallid Harrier	*Circus macrourus*	PM
						Montagu's Harrier	*Circus pygargus*	PM
						Goshawk	*Accipiter gentillis*	RB,WV?PM?
						Sparrowhawk	*Accipiter nisus*	PM,WV
						Levant Sparrowhawk*	*Accipiter brevipes*	PM

					English name	Scientific name	Status
	✓				Common Buzzard	*Buteo buteo*	PM,WV
✓					Long-legged Buzzard*	*Buteo rufinus*	WV,PM,RB
					Rough-legged Buzzard*	*Buteo lagopus*	AV
					Lesser Spotted Eagle*	*Aquila pomarina*	PM
					Spotted Eagle*	*Aquila clanga*	AV
					Imperial Eagle*	*Aquila heliaca*	RB,PM?
					Golden Eagle*	*Aquila chrysaetos*	AV
					Booted Eagle*	*Hieraaetus pennatus*	PM
					Bonelli's Eagle	*Hieraaetus fasciatus*	RB,PM
					Osprey	*Pandion haliaetus*	PM
					Lesser Kestrel	*Falco naumanni*	PM,WV
✓	✓				Kestrel	*Falco tinnunculus*	RB,PM,WV
					Red-footed Falcon	*Falco vespertinus*	PM
					Merlin	*Falco columbarius*	PM,WV
					Hobby	*Falco subbuteo*	MB,PM
					Eleonora's Falcon	*Falco eleonorae*	MB,PM
					Sooty Falcon*	*Falco concolor*	AV
					Lanner*	*Falco biarmicus*	AV
					Saker	*Falco cherrug*	PM
	✓				Peregrine	*Falco peregrinus*	RB,PM,WV
✓	✓				Chukar	*Alectoris chukar*	RB
✓	✓				Black Francolin	*Francolinus francolinus*	RB
					Quail	*Coturnix coturnix*	PM,SU
	✓				Water Rail	*Rallus aquaticus*	WV,PM,OB
					Spotted Crake	*Porzana porzana*	PM
					Little Crake	*Porzana parva*	PM,WV
					Baillon's Crake*	*Porzana pusilla*	PM,OB
					Corncrake	*Crex crex*	PM
✓					Moorhen	*Gallinula chloropus*	PM,WV,OB
					Allen's Gallinule*	*Porphyrula alleni*	AV
					Purple Gallinule*	*Porphyrio porphyrio*	AV
✓	✓				Coot	*Fulica atra*	WV,PM,OB
					Common Crane	*Grus grus*	PM
					Demoiselle Crane	*Anthropoides virgo*	PM
					Little Bustard*	*Tetrax tetrax*	AV
					Houbara Bustard*	*Chlamydotis undulata*	AV
					Great Bustard*	*Otis tarda*	AV
					Oystercatcher	*Haematopus ostralegus*	PM
					Black-winged Stilt	*Himantopus himantopus*	PM,OB
					Avocet	*Recurvirostra avosetta*	PM,WV
					Stone Curlew	*Burhinus oedicnemus*	RB,PM,WV
					Cream-coloured Courser*	*Cursorius cursor*	PM
					Collared Pratincole	*Glareola pratincola*	PM
					Oriental Pratincole*	*Glareola maldivarum*	AV
					Black-winged Pratincole	*Glareola nordmanni*	PM
					Little Ringed Plover	*Charadrius dubius*	PM,OB
					Ringed Plover	*Charadrius hiaticula*	PM,WV
					Kittlitz's Plover*	*Charadrius pecuarius*	AV
	✓				Kentish Plover	*Charadrius alexandrinus*	RB,PM,WV
	✓				Greater Sand Plover	*Charadrius leschenaultii*	PM,WV
					Caspian Plover*	*Charadrius asiaticus*	AV
					Dotterel*	*Charadrius morinellus*	PM

						English name	Scientific name	Status
✓	✓					Golden Plover	*Pluvialis apricaria*	WV,PM
						Grey Plover	*Pluvialis squatarola*	WV,PM
						Spur-winged Plover	*Holopterus spinosus*	PM,OB
						Sociable Plover*	*Vanellus gregarius*	AV
						White tailed Plover	*Vanellus leucurus*	PM
✓	✓					Lapwing	*Vanellus vanellus*	WV,PM
						Knot*	*Calidris canutus*	PM
						Sanderling	*Calidris alba*	PM,WV
						Little Stint	*Calidris minuta*	PM,WV
						Temminck's Stint	*Calidris temminckii*	PM
						Curlew Sandpiper	*Calidris ferruginea*	PM
						Dunlin	*Calidris alpina*	PM,WV
						Broad-billed Sandpiper*	*Limicola falcinellus*	PM
						Ruff	*Philomachus pugnax*	PM,WV
						Jack Snipe	*Lymnocryptes minimus*	PM
	✓					Common Snipe	*Gallinago gallinago*	PM,WV
						Great Snipe	*Gallinago media*	PM
						Woodcock	*Scolopax rusticola*	WV
						Black-tailed Godwit	*Limosa limosa*	PM,WV
						Bar-tailed Godwit*	*Limosa lapponica*	PM
						Whimbel	*Numenius phaeopus*	PM
						Slender-billed Curlew*	*Numenius tenuirostris*	AV
	✓					Curlew	*Numenius arquata*	PM,WV
						Spotted Redshank	*Tringa erythropus*	PM
						Common Redshank	*Tringa totanus*	WV,PM
						Marsh Sandpiper	*Tringa stagnatilis*	PM
						Greenshank	*Tringa nebularia*	PM,WV
	✓					Green Sandpiper	*Tringa ochropus*	PM,WV
						Wood Sandpiper	*Tringa glareola*	PM
						Terek Sandpiper*	*Xenus cinereus*	PM
✓	✓					Common Sandpiper	*Actitis hypoleucos*	PM,WV
✓						Turnstone	*Arenaria interpres*	PM
						Red-necked Phalarope	*Phalaropus lobatus*	PM
						Arctic Skua*	*Stercorarius parasiticus*	PM
						Great Black-headed Gull*	*Larus ichthyaetus*	OV
✓						Mediterranean Gull	*Larus melanocephalus*	PM,WV
✓	✓					Little Gull	*Larus minutus*	WV,PM
	✓					Black-headed Gull	*Larus ridibundus*	WV,PM
	✓					Slender-billed Gull	*Larus genei*	PM,WV
						Audouin's Gull	*Larus audouinii*	RB
						Common Gull	*Larus canus*	WV
✓	✓					Lesser Black-backed Gull	*Larus fuscus*	PM,WV
						Herring Gull*	*Larus argentatus*	AV
✓	✓					Yellow-legged Gull	*Larus cachinnans*	RB,WV,PM
						Armenian Gull*	*Larus armenicus*	WV,PM
						Great Black-backed Gull*	*Larus marinus*	AV
						Kittiwake*	*Rissa tridactyla*	AV
						Gull-billed Tern	*Sterna nilotica*	PM
						Caspian Tern	*Sterna caspia*	PM
✓	✓					Sandwich Tern	*Sterna sandvicensis*	WV,PM
						Common Tern	*Sterna hirundo*	PM,WV
						Arctic Tern*	*Sterna paradisaea*	AV

					English name	Scientific name	Status
					Little Tern	*Sterna albifrons*	PM
					Whiskered Tern	*Chlidonias hybridus*	PM
					Black Tern	*Chlidonias niger*	PM
					White-winged Black Tern	*Chlidonias leucopterus*	PM
					Black-bellied Sandgrouse*	*Pterocles orientalis*	RB,PM?
					Pin-tailed Sandgrouse	*Pterocles alchata*	NRTC
✓	✓				Rock Dove	*Columba livia*	RB
					Stock Dove	*Columba oenas*	WV,PM
✓	✓				Woodpigeon	*Columba palumbus*	RB,WV
	✓				Collared Dove	*Streptopelia decaocta*	RB,PM
					Turtle Dove	*Streptopelia turtur*	PM,MB
					Laughing Dove*	*Streptopelia senegalensis*	AV
					Great-spotted Cuckoo	*Clamator glandarius*	PM,MB
					Didric Cuckoo*	*Chrysococcyx caprius*	AV
					Cuckoo	*Cuculus canorus*	PM,OB?
					Barn Owl	*Tyto alba*	RB
					Scops Owl	*Otus scops*	RB,PM,MB?
					Little Owl	*Athene noctua*	RB
					Long-eared Owl	*Asio otus*	RB,WV,PM
					Short-eared Owl	*Asio flammeus*	PM,WV
					Nightjar	*Caprimulgus europaeus*	PM,MB
					Common Swift	*Apus apus*	PM,MB
					Pallid Swift	*Apus pallidus*	PM,MB
					Alpine Swift	*Apus melba*	MB,PM
					Little Swift*	*Apus affinis*	AV
					White-breasted Kingfisher*	*Halcyon smyrnensis*	WV
					Common Kingfisher	*Alcedo atthis*	PM,WV
					Pied Kingfisher	*Ceryle rudis*	WV
					Blue-cheeked Bee-eater	*Merops persicus*	PM
					European Bee-eater	*Merops apiaster*	PM,MB
					Roller	*Coracias garrulus*	PM,MB
	✕				Hoopoe	*Upupa epops*	PM,MB
					Wryneck	*Jynx torquilla*	PM,WV
					Desert Lark*	*Ammomanes deserti*	AV
					Dupont's Lark*	*Chersophilus duponti*	AV
					Calandra Lark	*Melanocorypha calandra*	RB,PM,WV?
					Bimaculated Lark	*Melanocorypha bimaculata*	PM
					Short-toed Lark	*Calandrella brachydactyla*	MB,PM
					Lesser Short-toed Lark*	*Calandrella rufescens*	PM,WV
✓	✓				Crested Lark	*Galerida cristata*	RB,PM,WV?
✓	✓				Woodlark	*Lullula arborea*	RB,WV,PM?
✓	✓				Skylark	*Alauda arvensis*	WV,PM
					Shore Lark*	*Eremophila alpestris*	AV
	✕				Sand Martin	*Riparia riparia*	PM
✓	✓				Crag Martin	*Ptyonoprogne rupestris*	RB,PM
	✓				Swallow	*Hirundo rustica*	MB,PM
					Red-rumped Swallow	*Hirundo daurica*	MB,PM
	✓				House Martin	*Delichon urbica*	MB,PM
					Richard's Pipit*	*Anthus novaeseelandiae*	PM
					Tawny Pipit	*Anthus campestris*	PM
					Long-billed Pipit*	*Anthus similis*	AV
					Olive-backed Pipit*	*Anthus hodgsoni*	AV

81

					English name	Scientific name	Status
					Tree Pipit	*Anthus trivialis*	PM
✓	✓				Meadow Pipit	*Anthus pratensis*	WV,PM
✓					Red-throated Pipit	*Anthus cervinus*	PM,WV
	✓				Water Pipit	*Anthus spinoletta*	PM,WV
					Yellow Wagtail	*Motacilla flava*	PM,MB
					Black-headed Wagtail	*Motacilla flava feldegg*	MB,PM
					Citrine Wagtail	*Motacilla citreola*	PM
✓	✓				Grey Wagtail	*Motacilla cinerea*	WV,PM,OB?
✓	✓				White Wagtail	*Motacilla alba*	WV,PM,OB
					Waxwing*	*Bombycilla garrulus*	AV
					Dipper*	*Cinclus cinclus*	EX
✓	✓				Wren	*Troglodytes troglodytes*	RB
					Dunnock	*Prunella modularis*	WV,PM?
					Rufous Bush Robin*	*Cercotrichas galactotes*	PM
✓	✓				Robin	*Erithacus rubecula*	WV,PM
					Thrush Nightingale	*Luscinia luscinia*	PM
					Nightingale	*Luscinia megarhynchos*	MB,PM
					Bluethroat	*Luscinia svecica*	PM,WV
					Red-flanked Bluetail*	*Tarsiger cyanurus*	AV
					White-throated Robin*	*Irania gutturalis*	AV
✓	✓				Black Redstart	*Phoenicurus ochuros*	WV,PM
					Common Redstart	*Phoenicurus phoenicurus*	PM
	✓				Whinchat	*Saxicola rubetra*	PM
✓	✓				Stonechat	*Saxicola torquata*	WV,PM
					Pied Stonechat*	*Saxicola caprata*	AV
	✓				Isabelline Wheatear	*Oenanthe isabellina*	PM
	✓				Northern Wheatear	*Oenanthe oenanthe*	PM
					Cyprus Pied Wheatear	*Oenanthe cypriaca*	MB
					Pied Wheatear*	*Oenanthe pleschanka*	AV
					Black-eared Wheatear**	*Oenanthe hispanica*	PM
					Desert Wheatear	*Oenanthe deserti*	PM
✓	✓				Finsch's Wheatear	*Oenanthe finschii*	WV,PM
					Red-tailed Wheatear*	*Oenanthe xanthroprymna*	AV
					Mourning Wheatear*	*Oenanthe lugens*	AV
					Hooded Wheatear*	*Oenanthe monacha*	AV
					White-crowned Wheatear*	*Oenanthe leucopyga*	AV
					Rock Thrush	*Monticola saxatilis*	PM
					Blue Rock Thrush	*Monticola solitarius*	RB,WV,PM
					Ring Ouzel	*Turdus torquatus*	PM,WV
✓	✓				Blackbird	*Turdus merula*	WV,PM,OB?
					Dusky Thrush*	*Turdus naumanni*	AV
✓					Fieldfare	*Turdus pilaris*	WV
✓	✓				Song Thrush	*Turdus philomelos*	WV,PM
					Redwing	*Turdus iliacus*	WV,PM
					Mistle Thrush	*Turdus viscivorus*	WV,PM
✓	✓				Cetti's Warbler	*Cettia cetti*	RB
✓	✓				Fan-tailed Warbler	*Cisticola juncidis*	RB
					Graceful Warbler*	*Prinia gracilis*	AV
					Grasshopper Warbler*	*Locustella naevia*	AV
					River Warbler*	*Locustella fluviatilis*	PM
					Savi's Warbler*	*Locustella luscinioides*	PM
					Moustached Warbler	*Acrocephalus melanopogon*	WV

				English name	Scientific name	Status
				Sedge Warbler	*Acrocephalus schoenobaenus*	PM
				Marsh Warbler*	*Acrocephalus palustris*	PM
				Reed Warbler	*Acrocephalus scirpaceus*	MB,PM
				Great Reed Warbler	*Acrocephalus arundinaceus*	PM,OB
				Basra Reed Warbler*	*Acrocephalus griseldis*	AV
				Olivaceous Warbler	*Hippolais pallida*	MB,PM
				Olive-tree Warbler	*Hippolais olivetorum*	PM
				Icterine Warbler**	*Hippolais icterina*	PM
✓	✓			Spectacled Warbler	*Sylvia conspicillata*	RB
				Subalpine Warbler**	*Sylvia cantillans*	PM
✓	✓			Sardinian Warbler	*Sylvia melanocephala*	WV,RB,PM?
✓	✓			Cyprus Warbler	*Sylvia melanothorax*	RB
				Rüppell's Warbler**	*Sylvia rueppelli*	PM
				Desert Warbler*	*Sylvia nana*	AV
				Orphean Warbler	*Sylvia hortensis*	PM
				Barred Warbler	*Sylvia nisoria*	PM
				Lesser Whitethroat	*Sylvia curruca*	PM
				Common Whitethroat	*Sylvia communis*	PM
				Garden Warbler	*Sylvia borin*	PM
✓	✓			Blackcap	*Sylvia atricapilla*	PM,WV,OB?
				Yellow-browed Warbler*	*Phylloscopus inornatus*	AV
				Dusky Warbler*	*Phylloscopus fuscatus*	AV
				Bonelli's Warbler**	*Phylloscopus bonelli*	PM
				Wood Warbler	*Phylloscopus sibilatrix*	PM
✓	✓			Chiffchaff	*Phylloscopus collybita*	PM,WV
				Willow Warbler	*Phylloscopus trochilus*	PM
				Goldcrest	*Regulus regulus*	WV
				Firecrest*	*Regulus ignicapillus*	AV
				Spotted Flycatcher	*Muscicapa striata*	MB,PM
				Red-breasted Flycatcher*	*Ficedula parva*	PM
				Semi-collared Flycatcher**	*Ficedula semitorquata*	PM
				Collared Flycatcher	*Ficedula albicollis*	PM
				Pied Flycatcher**	*Ficedula hypoleuca*	PM
				Bearded Tit	*Panurus biarmicus*	WV
✓	✓			Coal Tit	*Parus ater*	RB
✓	✓			Great Tit	*Parus major*	RB
				Wallcreeper	*Tichodroma muraria*	WV
	✓			Short-toed Treecreeper	*Certhia brachydactyla*	RB
				Penduline Tit	*Remiz pendulinus*	WV,OB
				Golden Oriole	*Oriolus oriolus*	PM,MB
				Isabelline Shrike*	*Lanius isabellinus*	AV
				Red-backed Shrike	*Lanius collurio*	PM
				Lesser Grey Shrike	*Lanius minor*	PM
				Great Grey Shrike*	*Lanius excubitor*	AV
				Woodchat Shrike	*Lanius senator*	PM,OB
				Masked Shrike	*Lanius nubicus*	MB,PM
✓	✓			Jay	*Garrulus glandarius*	RB
✓	✓			Magpie	*Pica pica*	RB,WV
✓	✓			Jackdaw	*Corvus monedula*	RB,WV
				Rook	*Corvus frugilegus*	WV
✓	✓			Hooded Crow	*Corvus corone*	RB
	✓			Raven	*Corvus corax*	RB

						English name	Scientific name	Status
	✓					Starling	*Sturnus vulgaris*	WV,PM
						Rose-coloured Starling	*Sturnus roseus*	PM
✓	✓					House Sparrow	*Passer domesticus*	RB,PM,WV?
✓	✓					Spanish Sparrow	*Passer hispaniolensis*	RB,PM,WV
						Dead Sea Sparrow	*Passer moabiticus*	SU
						Tree Sparrow	*Passer montanus*	WV
						Pale Rock Sparrow*	*Petronia brachydactyla*	AV
						Rock Sparrow*	*Petronia petronia*	AV
✓	✓					Chaffinch	*Fringilla coelebs*	RB,PM,WV
✓						Brambling*	*Fringilla montifringilla*	WV
						Red-fronted Serin*	*Serinus pusillus*	AV
✓	✓					Serin	*Serinus serinus*	RB,WV,PM
✓	✓					Greenfinch	*Carduelis chloris*	RB,WV,PM
✓	✓					Goldfinch	*Carduelis carduelis*	RB,WV,PM
	✓					Siskin	*Carduelis spinus*	WV
✓	✓					Linnet	*Carduelis cannabina*	AV ????
						Common Redpoll*	*Carduelis flammea*	RB,WV
✓	✓					Common Crossbill	*Loxia curvirostra*	PM
						Trumpeter Finch*	*Bucanetes githagineus*	AV
						Scarlet Rosefinch*	*Carpodacus erythrinus*	AV
	✓					Hawfinch	*Coccothraustes coccothraustes*	WV
						Pine Bunting*	*Emberiza leucocephalos*	AV
						Yellowhammer*	*Emberiza citrinella*	WV
						Rock Bunting*	*Emberiza cia*	PM,WV?
						Cinereous Bunting*	*Emberiza cineracea*	PM
						Ortolan Bunting	*Emberiza hortulana*	PM
						Cretzschmar's Bunting	*Emberiza caesia*	MB,PM
						Yellow-breasted Bunting*	*Emberiza aureola*	AV
	✓					Reed Bunting	*Emberiza schoeniclus*	WV
						Black-headed Bunting	*Emberiza melanocephala*	MB,PM
✓	✓					Corn Bunting	*Miliaria calandra*	RB,PM,WV

NOTES

NOTES

NOTES

LONDON CAMERA EXCHANGE
WINCHESTER

Established specialists for over 50 years in optical products.
Our commitment to our customers is to offer:

THE BEST ADVICE, THE BIGGEST CHOICE and THE LOWEST PRICES

Phone us last and see how we score against the rest !!

TELESCOPES   NIGHTSIGHTS

BINOCULARS   MONOCULARS   CAMERAS

CAMCORDERS   DIGITAL CAMERAS

ADVANCED PHOTO SYSTEM

COMPETITIVELY PRICED PROCESSING

15 THE SQUARE, WINCHESTER. SO23 9ES.

MAIL ORDER HOTLINE
01962 866203
FAX 01962 840978